aircraft illustrated
ANNUAL 1984

£3.95

Cover: Royal Navy Sea Harrier FRS1s of three of the squadrons based at RNAS Yeovilton, Somerset seen in the new dark grey colour scheme adopted in late-1982; the nearest aircraft carries the markings of No 800 Naval Air Squadron, the centre aircraft is from No 801 NAS and the third Sea Harrier is from No 899 NAS. *Crown Copyright, Royal Navy*

Below: A DC-9 srs 34, EC-DGC *Castillo de Sotomayor,* of the Spanish airline Aviacion y Comercio SA – Aviaco. *McDonnell Douglas Corp*

aircraft illustrated ANNUAL 1984

Edited by Martin Horseman

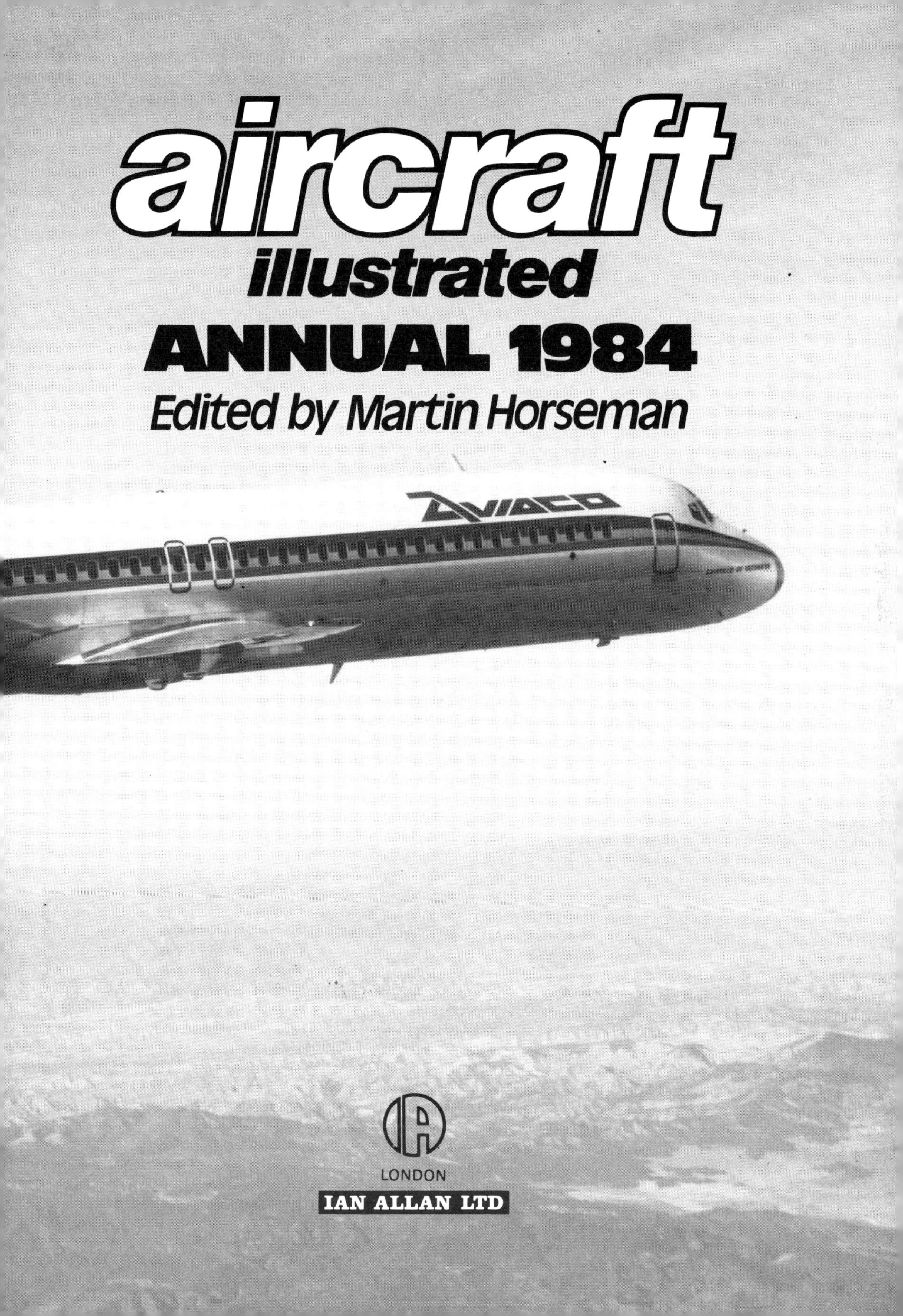

LONDON

IAN ALLAN LTD

First published 1983

ISBN 0 7110 1305 5

Published by Ian Allan Ltd, Shepperton, Surrey; and printed by Ian Allan Printing Ltd at their works at Coombelands in Runnymede, England.

Below: **USAF A-7D Corsair IIs of the 124th Tactical Fighter Squadron/132nd Tactical Fighter Wing, Iowa Air National Guard, seen during their August-September 1979 deployment to the UK codenamed 'Coronet Stallion'.** *P. A. Rowlings*

Contents

RAF Germany....

and allied air forces

Of all the Royal Air Force formations available for NATO tasking, the forces assigned to RAF Germany are probably more closely integrated into the structure of NATO's Allied Command Europe than any other part of the Service. RAF Germany is responsible for Britain's main air contribution to the defence of the European mainland and while in peacetime the Command remains an autonomous component of the Royal Air Force, it trains and exercises continuously as part of the NATO formation, the Second Allied Tactical Air Force (2ATAF), to which it would be assigned in the event of war – along with units of the German, Belgian and Dutch Air Forces. Among the links that foster the contacts between RAF Germany squadrons and their counterparts in 2ATAF and other NATO air commands is the regular programme of exchange visits during which detachments from the respective units visit each other's bases for one to two weeks of combined operations. Some of the allied air force scenes which result are shown in this feature.

Left: Members of No 19 Squadron RAF and No 331 Squadron Royal Norwegian Air Force with their respective aircraft types, a Phantom FGR2 and F-16A, at No 19's home base, RAF Wildenrath, during a squadron exchange in August 1982.
All photos in this article: RAF Germany

Above: A flight plan discussion during the visit of the RNorAF squadron and involving Flt Lt Robin Russell of No 19 Squadron (left) and Capt Per Strommen of No 331 Squadron.

Right: RNorAF F-16A and RAF Phantom FGR2 outside one of No 19 Squadron's hardened aircraft shelters at RAF Wildenrath. The Norwegian squadron is home based at Bodo AB in Northern Norway.

Below: Exercise 'Summer Tiger' in July 1982 saw Puma HC1 helicopters of No 33 Squadron from RAF Gütersloh operating in the field with German Air Force UH-1D Iroquois – two of the UH-1Ds are seen here either side of No 33's 'DK', XW226, at a refuelling point near a German farmhouse.

Top: Two of 2ATAF's tactical reconnaissance aircraft types pictured together at RAF Laarbruch, where the Jaguar-equipped No 2 Squadron RAF hosted a visiting detachment of Mirage 5BRs from No 42 Squadron Belgian Air Force in October 1980. Whereas the Jaguar's reconnaissance sensors are carried in a large underfuselage pod, the recce version of the Mirage 5 is fitted with nose-mounted camera systems.

Above: A Jaguar of No 14 Squadron at RAF Brüggen leads two Portuguese Air Force Fiat G91s along the taxiway during a visit to RAF Germany by No 310 Squadron from Montijo AB, near Lisbon.

Above: This Jaguar quartet over RAF Brüggen comprised two aircraft of No 14 Squadron, in the lead and slot positions, plus two visiting French Air Force Jaguars on the 'wings' of the formation. The French Jaguars were from *Esc 1/7* based at St Dizier.

Right: No 14 Squadron in the picture again, this time with one of its Jaguars alongside a visiting Hellenic Air Force A-7H Corsair II at RAF Brüggen.

Above: A December 1980 view of a No 20 Squadron Jaguar at Bitburg, AB FRG during an exchange visit with a USAF unit in the adjoining 4ATAF area; No 20's hosts were the 525th Tactical Fighter Squadron of the 36th Tactical Fighter Wing, one of whose F-15 Eagles can be seen in the background climbing out after take-off.

Below: Another view of No 20 Squadron's 'CH' on the flightline at Bitburg, in company with a visiting F-15 Eagle of the 32nd TFS from Soesterberg, Netherlands.

The 'Flying Cannons'

Kenneth E. Wixey

WHEN Bell Aircraft Corporation's new single-seat fighter was publicly revealed on 9 February 1939, it was expected to cause something of a sensation in military aviation circles if its manufacturer's claims proved viable. Designated the XP-39 the prototype Bell Airacobra was reputed by the company to have a top speed in excess of 400mph, a cruising speed of 325mph, a service ceiling of over 36,000ft, a range of 1,000 miles plus and a gross weight of 6,000lb. The aircraft was intended as a 400mph pursuit type, and was to carry aloft, in addition to fuselage and wing-mounted machine-guns, one of the largest guns ever fitted to a single-seater up until that time. This weapon was a 37mm T-9 cannon mounted in the nose of the machine, and designed to fire through the centre of the propeller hub. The fitting of this gun in such a position was made possible by installing the 1,150hp Allison V-1710-17 supercharged, liquid-cooled engine aft of the cockpit, a situation which also placed the greatest weight close to the XP-39's centre of gravity thus allowing for better manoeuvrability.

This data was well publicised by Bell and prompted a rash of complimentary references in the American press. Some referred to the new fighter as the Air Corps' slim 'mosquito', others wrote of the first airplane built in the States capable of maintaining flight at speeds in excess of 400mph; one prominent newspaper pointed out that some observers believed the Bell fighter was able to outfly and destroy any other aircraft then in existence. These beliefs were very short-lived.

The Airacobra became a victim of circumstance, the difference between a fast, high-altitude prototype with a supercharged engine, unarmed (the actual XP-39 did not have armament fitted) and lightly laden, and the production P-39 – fully loaded for war with a weight increase of 30 per cent. An even greater contributory factor in destroying any hope of the Airacobra becoming a high-altitude interceptor, was a recommendation by the NACA to delete the aircraft's supercharger. Other alterations included re-positioning the radiator to the wing and fuselage centre-section, lowering the cockpit canopy line, the fitting of a carburettor scoop just aft of the cockpit, and fairings to completely cover the undercarriage legs when retracted into the underwing wheel wells. After these modifications had been made, the prototype was redesignated the XP-39B.

The US Army Air Corps ordered 13 pre-production machines for evaluation these being designated YP-39s, and one machine powered by the Allison V-1710-37 low-altitude engine was known as the YP-39A. The Army then decided that all P-39s should be fitted with the low-altitude engine and what had

Below: Bell P-39C Airacobras of the US Army Air Corps seen at Selfridge, Michigan in early-1941; the aircraft belonged to the 31st Pursuit Group, the first US unit to receive the type. *Unless otherwise credited, all photos: Bell Aerospace Textron*

Left: The prototype Bell XP-39 Airacobra. *Author's Collection*

Below: A Bell P-39D undergoing night gun-firing tests – a dramatic but contrived 'air-to-air' view.

Bottom: In the early days of P-39 design, Bell began development of a navalised version of their new fighter. This was the XFL-1, known as the Airabonita.

originally promised to be a potentially effective high-altitude fighter, was relegated to ground attack and low-altitude operations.

At the time of its inception the Airacobra was innovatory in concept with the unorthodox engine position, very heavy armament, and the inclusion of a tricycle undercarriage, which made the P-39 the first aircraft with this type of landing-gear to be ordered by the USAAC. The three-bladed airscrew was driven by an 8ft extension shaft comprising two 4ft long sections 2½ inches in diameter. This extension passed beneath the pilot's legs, and together with the rear-mounted engine, was viewed with some apprehension by pilots who could visualise being crushed by the mass of the engine in a crash, or caught in the confined space of the cockpit if any breakage occurred in the shaft and gears whipping round beneath their legs. In several crashes that were investigated, however, it was found the engine had remained in position, and the interior of the cockpit was relatively secure despite considerable damage to other sections of the aircraft.

The P-39 Airacobra was the second unorthodox design for a combat aircraft to emerge from Bell Aircraft Corp. After leaving Consolidated Aircraft in 1935, Lawrence D. Bell formed his own company at Buffalo, New York, and together with chief engineer Robert J. Woods, designed an unusual long-range fighter with a crew of five! This strange looking machine was powered by two Allison V-1710-13 engines mounted as pushers, and the armament of six guns included two 37mm T-9 cannon, one in each forward protrusion of the engine nacelles which were glazed, and housed a gunner apiece.

The XP-39 design which followed was far from strange-looking, however. With its polished all-metal surfaces, low-wing monoplane configuration and well streamlined contours, the new prototype single-seat fighter was certainly pleasing aesthetically. But with the advent of the Army YP-39s, the increase in weight

Right: P-39 Airacobra, designated P400, for the RAF but minus serial numbers.

Below right: An RAF Airacobra runs up its engine prior to a pre-delivery test flight.
Author's Collection

had an adverse effect on the design. Whereas the unarmed XP-39 weighed 6,204lb for take-off, the armed YP-39 Army evaluation machines weighed up to 7,235lb. The guns fitted to these YP-39s comprised the hub-mounted 37mm cannon with two 0.50in, and two 0.30in machine-guns synchronised to fire through the propeller arc from the top of the cowling.

The YP-39s were ordered in April 1939, but by the time they appeared in September 1940, a production order had been placed for 80 P-39s by the USAAC. The first 20 of these were P-39Cs, which retained the four cowling guns, but the remaining 60 aircraft were delivered as P-39Ds with four 0.30in machine-guns in the wings, leaving the two 0.50in guns in the cowling, and the big T-9 cannon still protruding from the propeller hub. The P-39Ds also had self-sealing leak-proof fuel tanks, protective armour for the pilot, specially strengthened glass windscreen, and provision to carry either long-range fuel tanks with a 225gal capacity, or a 500lb bomb load. These additions led to the P-39D having a gross take-off weight in excess of 8,200lb.

Several variants of the Airacobra were built including the P-39D-1 with a 20mm cannon in place of the 37mm gun, the P-39D-2 powered by the Allison V-1710-63, three XP-39Es for laminar flow wing trials, the P-39F fitted with a General Motors propeller instead of the Curtiss electric, the P-39G, P-39K and P-39M, all with technical modifications mainly concerning engine and propeller gears, the P-39L fitted with a modified nosewheel, and the P-39N – the first version to be built in large numbers. Powered by a 1,200hp Allison V-1710-85 engine, 2,095 of the P-39N were produced. But it was the P-39Q which was built in the greatest quantity of all, 4,905 of this variant being the bulk of the total 9,558 Airacobras produced. It was the P-39Q that had its four wing-mounted 0.30in guns replaced by two 0.50in guns fitted one beneath each mainplane. An earlier version known as the P400 was a British-ordered Bell Model 14 Airacobra retained and flown by the USAAC in British camouflage pattern and still carrying their intended RAF serial numbers.

The first American operational unit to receive Airacobras was the 31st Pursuit Group which employed its P-39s during the Army 'Carolina Manoeuvres' in 1941, and it was there that the 'Marston' metal runway was first used. Another unit, the 8th Pursuit Group, became the first to take the P-39 into action in the Pacific when it arrived at Port Moresby, New Guinea during April 1942, and was joined later by the 35th Fighter Group (after May 1942 the designation 'Pursuit' was changed to 'Fighter') as well as units of the RAAF. Together with P-40s, the Bell Airacobras took part in a number of battles, and early in 1943 were engaged in fierce air fighting over Wau as Australian and Japanese ground forces clashed below in a bitter struggle. On one day alone in

Left: The first version of the Airacobra to be built in large numbers was the P-39N, seen here.

February 1943, USAAF and RAAF pilots claimed 24 Japanese aircraft out of 48 destroyed without loss to themselves.

Meanwhile the 347th Fighter Group, USAAF, had been receiving crated Airacobras for assembly at Tontouta airfield, New Caledonia, and one of the squadrons with 347th Group, the 67th Fighter Squadron, after several weeks training, left Tontouta for Guadalcanal on 22 August 1942. Among the Airacobras assembled at the New Caledonian base were a number of P400s, the aforementioned British version retained by the USAAC and still sporting their British pattern camouflage and serial numbers (BW108-BW183). Other crates contained P-39s built to US Army contracts, including P-39D-1s armed, like the P400s, with a 20mm cannon in the hub instead of the bigger 37mm gun.

The day after the 67th Squadron arrived at Guadalcanal, two of its pilots shared in the destruction of a Japanese 'Zero' fighter, but in most cases, the Airacobra was no match for the agile Mitsubishi A6M, especially at altitude. However, combat over the Guadalcanal area was usually confined to altitudes below 10,000ft as enemy aircraft operated mainly in covering naval task forces, and under these conditions the Airacobras could cope. At higher altitudes, pilots reported the P-39s lacking in the manoeuvrability required for aerial combat above 15,000ft.

Despite its shortcomings, however, the Airacobra was to win some acclaim in its low-altitude ground attack role. The ability to take punishment, whether in battle or in bad landings, was an asset to the P-39 and as well as carrying out low-level strafing missions the type was a proficient dive-bomber. When the 67th Squadron trained for the dive-bombing role they carried 100lb water-filled practice bombs diving at speeds in excess of 400mph; the recommended dive speed in the aircraft manuals was actually 475mph IAS. When fully armed for a dive-bombing sortie, the Airacobras carried either a 100, 350 or 500lb bomb in addition to the normal gun armament. To obtain greater accuracy in their attacks, pilots on dive-bombing missions often pulled out at very low-level; on one occasion, after a P-39D-2 had scored a direct hit on a Japanese cruiser, the pilot – Lt Jacobson operating out of Guadalcanal – flattened out only 40ft above the sea. US Army pilots in the Pacific were enthusiastic regarding the P-39's role as a ground attack aircraft, even if its intended function as an interceptor did leave much to be desired. In the event, the USAAF operated the Airacobras from 1941 until more advanced types appeared, and the 347th Fighter Group became the last unit in the Pacific to change its P-39s for Lockheed P-38 Lightnings, during August 1944.

Early in its combat career the Airacobra operated from the Aleutian Islands after the Japanese attack on the end of the Alaska Peninsula at Dutch Harbour in

June 1941. They flew with the 54th Fighter Group which included the 42nd, 56th and 57th Fighter Squadrons operating from Kodiak, Adak Island and Nome on the Seward Peninsula. An attack was mounted by the Americans against the Japanese on the Island of Kiska, and during the fighting the 54th Group pilots claimed 20 enemy aircraft destroyed for the loss of one P-39.

Quite a number of the original P400 British Airacobras re-acquired by the USAAF flew training missions in England up until December 1942, but during that month and January 1943, the aircraft were moved to North Africa to operate with the US 12th Air Force mostly on close-support missions. The 332nd Fighter Group in Italy also flew Airacobras, and in late-1944 was the last USAAF unit to change its P-39s for P-38 Lightnings.

Meanwhile Great Britain had become interested in the Airacobra, and the performance figures realised by the prototype XP-39 no doubt influenced the British Direct Purchasing Commission when they placed an order during April 1940 for 675 Bell Model 14s to be named the Caribou (later changed to the American nomenclature of Airacobra in July 1941). The British order, which included 200 machines originally ordered by France before the German advance, was provisionally allotted in four batches i.e., 170 (AH570-AH739), 121 (AP264-AP384), 84 (BW100-BW183) and 300 (BX135-BX434).

In the event, the Airacobra proved unsatisfactory in RAF service owing to limited operational capabilities at altitude, the seepage of carbon-monoxide into the cockpit after firing the nose guns, a bad time-lag encountered when loading or unloading the machine-guns and other armament problems, the impracticability of formation take-offs and landings because of the Airacobra's tendency to swing creating difficulties in regaining the planned flight path, and serious faults with the compass. Only one RAF unit, No 601 (County of London) Squadron was equipped with the Airacobra, converting from Hurricanes in September 1941. The American fighters served for only a short time with the squadron, during which they made four operational sorties. These took place between 9 and 11 October 1941 and took the form of low-level attacks ('rhubarbs' in RAF parlance) by aircraft working in pairs, and directed at targets along the French coast including an enemy trawler and some barges. By December, the Airacobras had been taken off operations and No 601 Squadron re-equipped with Spitfires somewhat thankfully.

A point of interest is the fact that while No 601 Squadron was flying its Airacobras from Duxford (the operations in October were mounted by detachments from RAF Manston in Kent), a group of Russian pilots arrived to try out the P-39s and they seemed impressed with the aircraft as a ground attack type. This was just

Below: A P-39N of the US Army Air Force; in all, 2,095 machines of this version were produced.

as well because instructions were issued that as a consequence of Russia's involvement on the side of the Allies since June 1941, those Airacobras which had already arrived in Britain, many still in their crates, were to be shipped on to Russia. The remainder of the British order mostly served with the USAAC as previously mentioned. The original Russian consignment was followed by a large number of P-39N and P-39Q variants, and altogether 4,746 Airacobras were received by the Soviet Air Force during World War 2. The type proved very popular with the Russian pilots who nicknamed it 'Little Shaver' – Soviet Air Force slang for ground-strafing.

One British Airacobra, AH574, was used by the Royal Navy for trials, and it is believed this machine was later fitted with an arrester hook at RAE Farnborough for on deck landing trials. This aircraft survived the war and was observed at Farnborough as late as 1948.

Later in the war, the Free French Air Force began to receive a number of P-39s, the first unit to be so equipped being *GC III/6* in April 1943. They flew P-39Ns and were followed by *GC I/4, GC I/5, GC III/5* and, according to some sources, *GC II/3*. One unit, *GC II/6*, was disbanded under the Vichy regime, but later reformed with P-39Ns again as *GC II/6* 'Travail' *(3eme Escadrille Forces Aériennes Francaises Libres)* in 1943. The Free French P-39Ns and Qs operated first as coastal patrol aircraft in North Africa, then flew on close support missions over Southern France and Italy until the end of the war in Europe.

A small number of P-39s found their way into the Portuguese Air Force after making forced landings in Portugal. These were painted in a top surface camouflage of brown and green, light grey undersurfaces with the usual Portuguese markings on wings and fuselages. Propeller hubs were in yellow and unit codes and serials in light grey. Some P-39Ns are also known to have served with the Italian Co-Belligerent Air Force in Yugoslavia during 1944.

A few P-39Qs survived the war to become civilianised, some having modifications added in the form of ventral or dorsal fins. One or two were converted into two-seaters known as the TP-39, one such machine being registered as N63813; another two-seat TP-39 was flying in Peru during the late-1950s. A majority of the civil P-39s in the United States were used for sport flying, and often flew with their rudders gaily bedecked with coloured chequers as well as sporting other bright insignia associated with air racing.

Returning to the early days of the P-39 design, Bell Aircraft also began development of a navalised version of their new fighter. Designated the XFL-1, and named the Airabonita, the Navy machine was similar in concept to the P-39 with its rear-mounted engine. However, it differed in having a conventional tailwheel in place of the nosewheel as fitted to the P-39, and the airframe was designed to withstand the extra stresses encountered by carrier-borne aircraft on embarked operations. A heat insulated-type firewall was provided at the forward end of the engine compartment, while the rear part was closed off by a metal bulkhead. Excepting the fabric-covered ailerons and moveable tail surfaces, the XFL-1 was of all-metal construction and flush riveting was employed wherever possible. Power was provided by a 1,150hp Allison XV-1710-6, 12 cylinder Vee, liquid-cooled engine driving a controllable-pitch Curtiss electric type propeller by means of an extension shaft. Prestone radiators were were fitted beneath the wings on the XFL-1 while the carburettor air intake, which was of the ram type, featured a cold-air scoop located aft of the cockpit on the top fuselage centre-line.

The proposed armament, never installed, comprised two 0.30in machine-guns and one 0.50in gun mounted in the forward fuselage (the 0.50in gun to fire through the propeller hub), or the two 0.30in guns to be mounted in the wings and either a 0.50in gun or 37mm cannon to be situated in the propeller hub. In addition, there was provision to carry up to 40 small bombs in five underwing bomb containers when fitted.

The Airabonita was equipped also with flotation gear, a life raft was carried just behind the pilot to the right, and emergency equipment for use in a forced 'ditching' included rations, oxygen bottle, Very pistol, flares, smoke grenades, drinking water and a flashlight. The Bell XFL-1 made its first flight on 13 May 1940, but later, after failing to pass its US Navy carrier qualification trials, the single prototype was dispensed with, and no further development of the type was undertaken.

One other improved variant of the P-39 was, however, to prove itself as a ground-attack aircraft. In the early design stages of the Airacobra, work was already in progress with a new wing having an aerofoil which would result in laminar flow. During April 1941, an order was placed for two prototype aircraft fitted with the new style wing, their designation to be the XP-39E. Two months later a second contract was signed, this time for two prototypes of a new design altogether which would incorporate the new laminar-flow wing. The result was the first flight, on 7 December 1942, of the XP-63 powered by a 1,325hp Allison V-1710-47 engine, still retained in the same position behind the pilot. Two XP-63s were built to be followed by a third prototype XP-63A, this aircraft making its initial flight on 26 April 1943 powered by a 1,500hp Allison V-1710-93.

In general layout the new fighter was very similar to its predecessor, the P-39, but had larger dimensions and a revised tail unit. The gun armament was similar, and consisted of a 37mm cannon installed in the airscrew hub with two 0.50in guns in the forward fuselage; later versions had two 0.50in guns fitted beneath the wings. Production P-63A-1s could carry three 500lb bombs, and later models had their armoured protection increased.

Above: Successor to the P-39 was the P-63 Kingcobra, most of which were supplied to the Soviet Union for service with the Red Air Force.

Named the Kingcobra, the Bell P-63A series was modified until the P-63A-10 was replaced by the P-63C powered by the Allison V-1710-117 with water injection. One P-63D was built with a redesigned cockpit canopy and larger wing, but the P-63E which followed, although retaining the 'D' wing and Allison V-1710-109 engine as fitted to the P-63D, reverted to the original style of cockpit canopy. Only 13 P-63Es were completed. One P-63F was produced with further revision to the vertical tail surfaces, this machine having an Allison V-1710-135.

Although only serving with the USAAF chiefly as a 'restricted pursuit' aircraft, usually as a high-speed target machine, the majority of Kingcobras went to Russia for service with the Red Air Force. In fact the Soviet Union received 2,421 P-63s, most of which were flown on ground attack missions, a role they were to excel at in the hands of their Russian pilots as they attacked German forces on the Eastern Front. Quite a number of Kingcobras served with the Free French Air Force in World War 2, and with the *Armée de l'Air* in the immediate postwar years.

Also, like its predecessor, the Kingcobra became a civil sporting machine, several P-63C-5s being converted for racing, and as two-seaters. One such machine carried the civil registration N41964. Again, like the P-39, a number of P-63s were still flying in Peru during the late-1950s.

As a war machine, and in spite of its shortcomings as a high altitude fighter, Bell's unorthodox design proved its worth as a lethal ground attack aircraft, especially in the hands of Soviet pilots. Russia received over 4,700 P-39s, and the same source quotes a final figure of 2,900 P-63s, although this latter total does not tally with an official number noted in a later publication. This difference may be due possibly to the numbers of aircraft lost at sea while in convoy and en route for Russia, the official figure of 2,421 apparently quoting the number of P-63s actually received by the Red Air Force.

Meanwhile in the Pacific, North Africa and Italy, the USAAF had the use of an aircraft that would hold the fort until the rapidly expanding American war effort could supply more advanced types than the P-39. The Airacobra was available when it was desperately needed, and, together with the later Kingcobra, played an important stop-gap role which helped pave the way to eventual and total Allied victory in the East and West.

Bell P-39D Airacobra

Powerplant: One 1,150hp Allison V-1710-35 liquid-cooled engine.

Performance: Max speed, 335mph at 5,000ft, 360mph at 15,000ft.

Above: Bell P-63A Kingcobra of the USAAF.
Author's Collection

Climb rate: 5,000ft/1.9min, 20,000ft/9min.
Service ceiling: 32,100ft.
Range: clean, 600 miles at 10,000ft at 231mph or, with drop-tank, 1,100 miles at 196mph.
Weights: Empty, 5,4621b. Loaded (normal), 7,650lb, max take-off, 8,850lb.
Armament: One 37mm T-9 cannon firing through propeller hub, two 0.50in machine-guns in upper cowling, and four 0.30in machine-guns installed as pairs in outer wing panels.
Dimensions: Span, 34ft; length, 30ft 2in; height, 11ft 10in.

Bell XFL-1 Airabonita
Powerplant: One 1,150hp Allison XV-1710-6 liquid-cooled engine.
Performance: Max speed, 307mph at sea level, 336mph at 10,000ft.
Climb rate: 2,630ft/min.
Max range: 1,072 miles.
Weights: Empty, 5,161lb. Loaded, 7,212lb.
Armament (proposed only): One 0.50in machine-gun firing through propeller hub, and two 0.30in machine-guns in top cowling, or 37mm T-9 cannon or 0.50in machine-gun firing through propeller hub, and two wing-mounted 0.30in machine-guns. Provision for up to 40 small bombs to be carried beneath the wings.
Dimensions: Span, 35ft; length, 29ft 9in; height, 12ft 9in.

Bell P-63A-10 Kingcobra
Powerplant: One 1,500hp Allison V-1710-93 liquid-cooled engine.
Performance: Max speed, 361mph at 5,000ft, 410mph at 25,000ft.
Service ceiling: 43,000ft.
Range: normal, 450 miles; with extra capacity drop-tank, max of 2,200 miles at 177mph at 10,000ft.
Weights: Empty, 6,375lb. Loaded (gross take-off), 10,500lb.
Armament: One 37mm T-9 cannon firing through propeller hub, two 0.50in machine-guns in top cowling synchronised to fire through propeller arc, and two 0.50in machine-guns installed in underwing fairings. A total bomb load of 1,500lb could be carried, usually comprising three 500lb bombs.
Dimensions: Span, 38ft 4in; length, 32ft 8in; height, 12ft 7in.

Acknowledgement
The author wishes to acknowledge the generous assistance given in the preparation of this article by Bell Aerospace (Division of TEXTRON Inc) who also supplied the photographs.

Aircraft accidents in the 1930s

Acknowledgement

The assistance of Mr J. P. Griffin in the preparation of this article is gratefully acknowledged – *Ed.*

Below: The upturned wreckage of an Air France Loire et Oliver 213 mailplane on the outskirts of Croydon on 31 May 1934. The two crew of the LeO 213 died in the crash, which happened in the early morning when the aircraft took off for Paris from a mist-covered Croydon Airport, struck a wireless mast, hit several houses and buried itself into this front garden.

Below right: The instructor and student pilot escaped with minor injuries when this DH82A Tiger Moth, G-ADHV, from the De Havilland School of Flying crashed at Hatfield on 2 November 1935.

Bottom right: The remains of Airspeed AS6J Envoy I, G-ADBZ, in Whistler's Wood, Oxted, Surrey. Originally serving with North Eastern Airways, and named *Swaledale*, 'BZ' was leased to Air Dispatch Ltd at Croydon in 1936, and came to its untimely end here on 22 January 1937 after setting out on a flight to Paris.

FIVE decades ago the progress of air transport was periodically marred, as sadly it still is nowadays, by accidents to airliners flying the pioneering routes in Europe and elsewhere with their limited complements of passengers and mail. Civil air transport was still in its formative years during the 1930s and had yet to be supported by the enormous range of blind flying and navigation aids which have improved the safety record of the industry in the modern era. Nor was the evidence of aeroplanes' and crews' misfortunes in the face of adverse operating conditions limited to pictures of crumpled transport aircraft – the flying training schools and the fledging RAF suffered their share of mishaps. This collection of photographs, kindly made available by a reader of *Aircraft Illustrated*, offers mute testimony to the hazards of aviation in the inter-war years.

Above: This RAF Hawker Hart, K4963, crashed at Easton-on-the-Hill near Stamford on 27 November 1935 during a flight from RAF Wittering. The pilot, LAC MacDonald, was under training with No 11 Flying Training School and survived the accident by taking to his parachute, landing unhurt about a mile away from the crash.

Right: Firemen combing through the wreck of a KLM DC-2 airliner, PH-AKL *Lijster*, which came to grief in foggy conditions at Purley after taking off from Croydon on the morning of 9 December 1936. Among those killed in this accident was the autogyro pioneer, Sr Juan de la Cierva.

Above: This Avro Avian IV, G-AAAT, plunged into an orchard garden at Cheltenham on the evening of 21 September 1935. The pilot had a narrow escape as the aircraft broke down several trees before coming to earth upside down.

Below: Only a short career was enjoyed by this Blackburn B2 two-seat trainer; delivered to Flying Training Ltd at Hanworth, Middlesex in February 1936, the aircraft was written off on 17 August of the same year after crashing at Kingsbury.

Below: Duxford in 1982 – part of an impressive line-up outside the hangars with the latest arrival at that time, Vulcan B2, XJ824, on the extreme left.
Peter R. March and A. P. March

The Imperial War Museum

at Duxford

Peter R. March

THE construction of Duxford Airfield began in 1917, the worst year of World War 1 and the one in which the Germans made their first bombing raids by aircraft on the centre of London in broad daylight. The reaction of the British Government to those raids led to the creation in the following year of a new independent fighting service, the Royal Air Force, to improve the country's defence against bombing and to develop a counter-offensive against Germany. In that same year, 1917, Lloyd George's government also decided that there should be a national museum to collect, preserve and eventually to display the evidence of war. Thus 1917 saw the creation of the Imperial War Museum and the construction of Duxford Airfield. Some sixty years later it was this Museum which secured the permanent preservation of Duxford Airfield.

Duxford became a familiar name in 1940 when it played a vital role as a main base in the Battle of Britain. The 'Big Wing' tactics of Fighter Command's No 12 Group were especially connected with the base. Later in the war when the RAF went over to the offensive and the Americans arrived in force, Britain became a massive 'aircraft carrier' with many fighter and fighter-bomber squadrons based in East Anglia. Duxford was home for USAAF Thunderbolts and Mustangs with their brown-uniformed crews becoming very much part of the local scene.

After 1945 this rash of airfields began to vanish almost as rapidly as it had appeared. Duxford had a longer reprieve than most, having been returned to the RAF as a fighter base. But in 1961 its usefulness to the RAF with its ever-changing requirements was ultimately exhausted. A period of 43 years of continuous use came to an end.

Lest all should eventually vanish without trace the Imperial War Museum decided to preserve one of the historic Battle of Britain airfields in the same way as it has since preserved the last survivor of the Royal Navy's all-gun big ships, HMS *Belfast*. What seemed to be a natural choice was Duxford with its long history and architecturally significant buildings. Complicated negotiations were put in hand with the Government and Cambridgeshire Country Council which eventually came to a fruitful conclusion in 1971.

So the Imperial War Museum, with the help of the East Anglian Aviation Society commenced use of part of a hangar in September that year. The first aircraft to be restored was the Museum's P-51D Mustang, 44-73979, and the first exhibit to be flown in was Sea Vixen FAW2, XS576, in March 1972. In this way, Duxford Airfield became an integral part of the Imperial War Museum, preserved as an exhibit in its own right and the setting for a unique and large display of aircraft dating from the Royal Aircraft Factory BE2C of 1916 to the pre-production BAC Concorde of

Left: North American P-51D Mustang *Big Beautiful Doll*, in the markings of aircraft flown by the CO of the 78th Fighter Group USAAF from Duxford during WW2.

Below left: Restoration complete, the unique Royal Aircraft Factory RE8, F3556, in the IWM Collection.

Top right: Pre-production BAC/Aerospatiale Concorde 101, G-AXDN, on static display at Duxford.

Centre right: A view from the control tower, with the ex British Airways Super VC10, G-ASGC, nearest the camera.

Bottom right: The repainted Boeing B-29A Superfortress, s/n 44-61748, *Hawg Wild*.

1971, together with tanks, small vessels, guns and the larger paraphernalia of warfare. Alongside over 80 aircraft there are armoured fighting vehicles of German, British, Russian and American origin which help to tell the story of warfare over most of the years of this century.

The public were first able to see the new collection, which by then numbered 10 aircraft, at an air display in October 1973. In June 1976 Duxford, by then an integral part of the Imperial War Museum, was opened to the public for the first time on a daily basis. The numbers of visitors rose rapidly to nearly 400,000 in the 1980 season; in its first few years of opening, Duxford attracted a total of well over a million visitors. The number of aircraft on display had grown and many of the Museum's most interesting large exhibits, such as the coastal motor boat in which Lieutenant (later Captain) Augustus Agar RN won the VC in 1919 and the German *Jagdpanther* tank destroyer, went on public view for the first time.

In the same period the airfield buildings, neglected and vandalised in the years following the departure of the Royal Air Force, were restored by the Property Services Agency of the Department of the Enviroment. This has enabled the Museum to make considerable improvments in the displays and public facilites.

The largest single improvment in the accommodation availible for displays at Duxford was achieved in 1980 when the Museum arranged the dismantling of a Type T-2 hanger at Tempsford, Bedfordshire, and its re-erection, on a site previously occupied by a hangar of that type at Duxford. As well as record attendances and a new hangar, 1980 also saw the opening of the Museum's first permanent exhibitions. One, mounted with considerable help from the United States, illustrates the role and achievements of the United States Eighth Air Force, which operated from United Kingdom bases, including Duxford, from 1942 to 1945. The other, a photographic exhibition on the history of Duxford Airfield, helps to underline the importance of the airfield as an exhibit in itself, quite apart from the collections now displayed there.

The rapid development of Duxford as a major national museum stems from the unique relationships achieved between the Imperial War Museum, the Cambridgeshire County Council and the Duxford Aviation Society. The Society, which was formed in 1975, is a voluntary group of enthusiastic 'Friends' of

AIR LONDON

British airways

461748
TATES AIR FORCE

Above: De Havilland Sea Venom FAW21, XG613, in one of the Duxford hangar displays.

Below: Among the impressive collection of airliners built up by the Duxford Aviation Society are the former Monarch Airlines Bristol Britannia 312, G-AOVT, and . . .

Bottom: . . . an ex Cambrian Viscount 701, G-ALWF.

Left: Gloster Javelin FAW9, XH897; examples of the delta wing fighter were among the last aircraft to be based at Duxford, with No 64 Squadron, before the airfield was relinquished by the RAF in 1961.

Below: Avro Anson 1, N4877/G-AMDA.

Bottom: One of the more than 20 airworthy aircraft based at Duxford is this ex RAF Varsity T1, WJ945.

the IWM, which assists the Museum in many ways. In particular its members provide a great deal of manpower and skill in working on the various restoration projects amongst the Museum's collections. In addition the Society has built up an impressive collection of civil airliners, including a Viscount, Comet, Britannia, VC10 and perhaps most significant of all, the British pre-production Concorde G-AXDN which was flown into Duxford in August 1977, just before the construction of the M11 motorway which reduced the usable length of the runway by some 1,500ft.

In April 1977 the County Council acquired nearly 150 acres of the airfield, including the shortened runway, and concluded an agreement with the Imperial War Museum for the joint management of this land and activities at Duxford. This made it possible for flying to continue as an attraction for visitors to the airfield and for new acquisitions to continue to be flown in for the Museum. One of the most important of these was the B-29A Superfortress, 44-61748, which was donated by the United States Navy. After being restored to airworthy condition by a team of specialists working under the Museum's supervision it made the 6,600-mile flight from California to the United Kingdom via Newfoundland, Greenland and Iceland, arriving at Duxford on 2 March 1980.

Though some of the largest and most striking exhibits are displayed in the open, covered display areas amount to over 100,000 sq ft. There are also the following exhibitions: The history of Duxford Airfield, some 200 photographs illustrating the long and varied history of Royal Air Force Duxford; Armoured

Above right: Undergoing restoration to airworthy condition is a Bristol Bolingbroke IVT that formerly served with the Royal Canadian Air Force.

Right: Spad S7 biplane fighter, N4727V.

Below: Representing the *Luftwaffe* of WW2 is the Me163B Komet rocket fighter.

Warfare, photographs and equipment relating to the development of armoured fighting vehicles in the 20th century; The United States Eighth Air Force, models, uniforms, equipment, graphics and photographs recording the role and achievements of the US Eighth Air Force in World War 2; 9.2 inch coastal defence gun from Spur Battery, Gibraltar, two associated exhibitions illustrating the role of Gibraltar in the history of the British Empire, and how the gun was dismantled, transported and reassembled at Duxford by the Royal Engineers.

There are some two dozen airworthy aircraft based at Duxford which include Spitfire VC AR501, the first restored aircraft to fly from the airfield, various Harvards, Yakovlev C.11, Beech D17S Staggerwing, Tiger Moths, DH Dragon Rapide, Fiesler Storch, Varsity, Boeing B-17G Fortress and Broussard. There is also a similar number of interesting types under restoration to fly, including a Bristol Bolingbroke IVT, Hawker Sea Hurricane I, P-51D Mustang and Anson C19. These aircraft are owned in the main by private individuals or groups who are permitted the use of the facilities at Duxford and in return allow their aircraft to go on display in the museum and where appropriate take part in the various Flying Days and Displays held during the summer months.

Plans for the further development of Duxford include the renovation of the former officers' mess, which, along with the the other buildings north of the A505 was allocated to the Museum in 1978. These will be used to provide new exhibition galleries and improved public facilities. The top priority of the Museum Trustees is the construction of a further new hangar large enough to accommodate and display the largest aircraft in the collection and in particular the B-29 Superfortress and the Concorde. It is hoped that this major project will be completed by the start of the new season in March 1984.

Top: Former US Air Force Convair VT-29B, s/n 0-17899.

Above: Another Duxford-based display aircraft is this F4U-7 Corsair in French Navy markings.

Duxford Airfield is situated on the A505 road, 8 miles south of Cambridge, next to Junction 10 on the M11 motorway. An express coach service operates daily to the airfield from Victoria Coach Station, London during the summer season. The Museum is open daily (except Good Friday and May Day Bank Holiday) from mid-March to the end of October from 11am to 5.30pm (or dusk if earlier). Flying Days and full Flying Displays are held approximately once a month through the season. For further details telephone Cambridge (0223) 833963.

Colour cameo: 1 The globetrotting BAe 146

Above: The BAe 146, G-SCHH, seen at Delhi in late-1982 during a stopover at Safdarjung, the city's old downtown airport. The aircraft, the fifth srs 100 and formerly registered G-BIAJ, staged through India on both outward and return journeys of its 51-day, 58,800-mile demonstration tour of Asia and Australasia which took place between 24 October-13 December 1982. *British Aerospace*

Below: The BAe 146's itinerary included eight days in Japan where, as at other locations on the tour, the aircraft was demonstrated to potential customer airlines, aviation officials, local agencies and the media. This view shows the 146 at Osaka, where a complete day was given over to noise measurements. The 146's lower noise level compared to twin-turboprops, twin- and tri-jets using the airport impressed local environmental agencies. *British Aerospace*

The first BAe 146, G-SSSH, at Hatfield on 20 May 1981 during the roll-out ceremonies marking the new airliner's public debut. *Allan Burney*

Above: In Australia the BAe 146 visited Perth, Canberra, Melbourne, Adelaide and Sydney, where the aircraft was pictured flying past the famous Harbour Bridge and Opera House. *British Aeropace*

Right: The BAe 146 in New Zealand and overflying Mount Cook airport's 5,000ft runway which lies near the base of the 12,000ft-high peak of the same name. In adverse, blustery conditions the 146 made a problem-free approach through the mountains to this remote airport. *British Aerospace*

Colour cameo: 2 Europe's widebody Airbus

Top: The Airbus Industrie flight test centre at Toulouse with a cluster of A300 Airbus widebody twin-jets linked to the building by the purpose-designed walkways. This facility, the so-called *abreuvoir* ('drinking-trough'), is used for the flight preparation and maintenance of Airbuses based at Toulouse prior to their delivery to the airlines, and it gives the pilots and engineers easy access to the aircraft. *Airbus Industrie*

Above: An A300 Airbus, D-AIAB, of the German airline Lufthansa landing at London Heathrow Airport. *British Aerospace, Hatfield*

The first A300 Airbus acquired by Laker Airways landing at Gatwick on 10 January 1981.
Graham Finch

An A300 Airbus in the markings of the Spanish airline Iberia seen at Orly Airport, Paris on 30 May 1981. *Denis Fleury*

Top: A view of the paint shop at Toulouse with an A300 being finished in the colours of the Belgian charter airline Trans European Airways. *Airbus Industrie*

Above: Olympic Airways' SX-BEB at London Heathrow Airport on 2 April 1979 when the airline inaugurated A300 Airbus services between Athens and London. *British Aerospace, Hatfield*

Colour cameo: 3 Museum masterpieces

Above: The Short Sandringham flying-boat *Southern Cross* owned by the Science Museum was moved from RNAS Lee-on-Solent to Southampton Docks on 1-2 March 1983, and the aircraft is seen here descending the slipway prior to being loaded on a Mexeflote barge for the journey. After dismantling for inspection and restoration, the Sandringham is to be reassembled and displayed at the new R. J. Mitchell Museum in Southampton from 1984. *The Science Museum*

Below: A mid-March 1983 view of the Bomber Command Museum's fully completed DH9A, F1010 (the story of the aircraft's restoration is told in the article beginning on page 66 – *Ed*). The 'Nine-Ack', virtually a new aircraft such was the scale of the restoration work, has been finished to the modification state pertaining in late-1918. Within days of the aircraft's completion at the RAF Museum's Restoration and Storage Centre at Cardington – where it was pictured in this view – the DH9A was derigged and transported to Hendon for reassembly in the Bomber Command Museum. *R. A. Nicholls*

Another RAF Museum masterpiece from Cardington is the Hanriot HD-1, painted in the markings of the *1e Escadrille, Aviation Militaire Belge*. R. A. Nicholls

A beautifully restored Douglas A-20K Havoc of the Brazilian *Museu Aeroespacial*, situated near Rio de Janeiro. In the space of three years, the A-20K was transformed from a vandalised relic found in a children's playground to this masterpiece of the restorer's art. *Major J. M. Monteiro*

Below: Junkers Ju52 on display at the Imperial War Museum, Duxford. *Andrew March*

Bottom: Spitfire Mk XVI, TB752, at RAF Manston after its restoration by the Medway Branch of the Royal Aeronautical Society.

Colour cameo: 4 The RAF 'Red Arrows'

Above: An aerial salute by The Royal Air Force 'Red Arrows' aerobatic team in their Gnat T1s to the new aircraft with which they were re-equipped in late-1979, the BAe Hawk T1. *British Aerospace, Kingston*

Below: The 'Red Arrows' with their Hawk T1s seen en route from the BAe plant at Bitteswell (where the aircraft were specially modified for display flying) to RAF Kemble on 15 November 1979. *British Aerospace, Kingston*

Two views of a pre-season training sortie by the RAF 'Red Arrows' on 10 February 1981. The photographs show the Hawk T1s of the team pulling up to the top of a loop in wineglass formation and at low-level in the delta formation introduced for the 1981 season.
Allan Burney

Colour cameo: 5 Sea Harrier scenes

Right: More than any other, the aircraft which made its mark during the Falklands campaign in 1982 was the BAe Sea Harrier FRS1. The Fleet Air Arm's first squadron to receive the Sea Harrier was No 700A Squadron, the Sea Harrier Intensive Flying Trials Unit, which formed at Yeovilton in mid-1979; one of No 700A's aircraft was pictured aboard the aircraft carrier HMS *Hermes* in November that year during a deployment aimed at familiarising the squadron and the carrier with the procedures for operating fixed-wing V/STOL aircraft at sea. This view of *Hermes'* flightdeck pre-dated the installation of the carrier's ski-jump take-off ramp.
British Aerospace, Kingston

Below: Sea Harrier FRS1, XZ454, carrying the fin markings (gold trident and crossed swords set in a white-edged crimson arrowhead) of No 800 Naval Air Squadron, the FAA's first front-line squadron to form on the Sea Harrier. No 800 NAS was commissioned at RNAS Yeovilton on 23 April 1980.
Crown Copyright, HMS Heron

Above: The second front-line squadron to be equipped with the Sea Harrier was No 801 NAS, which formed at Yeovilton on 28 January 1981 and commissioned a month later, on 26 February. One of the squadron's aircraft, flying from the carrier HMS *Invincible* during Exercise 'Ocean Venture' in August 1981, was pictured keeping an eye on a Soviet Tu-95 'Bear-D' reconnaissance aircraft over the North Atlantic. *Crown Copyright, No 801 Naval Air Squadron*

Below: A Sea Harrier FRS1 of No 899 Naval Air Squadron launching from the ski-jump ramp at Yeovilton. No 899 NAS was formed from No 700A Squadron to become the Sea Harrier headquarters and training squadron at Yeovilton, being commissioned there on 22 May 1980. This photograph, dating from May 1982, shows the aircraft in a medium sea grey/barley grey scheme with toned-down national and squadron markings, this providing a marked revision to the earlier camouflage of gloss-finished extra dark sea grey uppersurfaces and white undersurfaces exhibited by the Nos 800 and 801 NAS aircraft in the preceding photographs. *Crown Copyright, HMS* Heron

ROYAL NAVY
VL

Sea Harriers of the first two operational squadrons – Nos 800 and 899 Naval Air Squadrons.
Peter R. March

Below: Sea Harriers aboard HMS *Hermes* in April 1982 en route to their combat debut in the South Atlantic – alongside the carrier was the Type 22 frigate HMS *Broadsword*. The aircraft had been painted in an extra dark sea grey finish devoid of squadron markings. *Crown Copyright*

Bottom: Two Sea Harriers exhibiting the early-1983 semi-gloss camouflage finish of dark sea grey selected for the aircraft; the scheme includes small red and blue roundels with black serial numbers and aircraft codes – the further aircraft, 004, also carries the revised fin insignia of No 801 NAS.
Crown Copyright, HMS Heron

Colour cameo: 6 1,000 Islanders and Trislanders

Above: In early-1982 Pilatus Britten-Norman delivered the 1,000th BN2, thereby capping a remarkable 14-year period which had seen the delivery of 926 Islanders and Defenders, 72 Trislanders and two Turbine Islanders. This February 1978 picture shows a BN2A Islander, c/n G585, with the US registration N31MN awaiting delivery to Munz Northern Airlines at Nome, Alaska.
Simon R. P. Thomson

Below: A BN2A-27 Islander seen at Bembridge before delivery to the Romanian Flying School.
Simon R. P. Thomson

A BN2A-21 Defender of the Botswana Defence Force pictured on a pre-delivery test flight.
Simon R. P. Thomson

A colourful BN2A Mk III Trislander, G-AZLJ, of Aurigny Air Services Ltd seen at the States of Jersey Airport. *A. J. Wright*

Above: This Loganair Trislander, G-BBNL, served with the Scottish airline between 1973-80 and was subsequently redelivered to an operator in Columbia.

Below: A Trislander in the markings of Inter-Island Airways of the Seychelles. *Simon R. P. Thomson*

Colour cameo: 7 Westland Sea King

Above: A Westland Sea King HAS2 of No 824 Naval Air Squadron displays its armament of four torpedoes during a firepower demonstration conducted by aircraft from HMS *Ark Royal* in October 1978. No 824 NAS was the first operational Fleet Air Arm squadron to equip with Sea Kings, the HAS1 version, when it formed at RNAS Culdrose in February 1970.
Crown Copyright, Royal Navy

Left: A typical search and rescue scene, dating from February 1974, and involving a Royal Navy Sea King; in this instance the aircraft is an HAS 1, and the crew was about to start winching survivors from the lifeboat of a coastal vessel which has been abandoned in stormy weather.
Crown Copyright, Royal Navy

Two views of RAF Sea King HAR3s operating with No 202 Squadron; the picture below shows XZ594 of the squadron's A Flight hovering just above the apron at RAF Boulmer, Northumberland, while the photo at bottom illustrates an aircraft of C Flight from RAF Coltishall, Norfolk conducting winch practice over the North Sea. *Patrick Little* and *James A. Simpson*

DANGER
XZ595
ROYAL AIR FORCE
RESCUE
RAF
RESCUE

MARINE
SAR
89 50
DANGER

ROYAL NAVY
VC

DANGER
ROYAL NAVY

CU
DANGER
ROYAL NAVY
XV650

Left: A Sea King Mk 41 of the German Navy seen over Somerset during a pre-delivery test flight from Westland Aircraft's Yeovil base.
Westland Helicopters Ltd

Far left, centre: The troop transport and logistic support version of the Sea King is the HC Mk 4. Shown here is an HC4 of No 846 NAS operating in its primary role as a battlefield support and transport helicopter, and embarking Royal Marine commandos and their equipment during a winter exercise in North Norway. *Crown Copyright, Royal Navy*

Far left, bottom: The latest anti-submarine version of the Sea King to enter Royal Navy service is the HAS5, and this view shows the prototype aircraft, XZ916 – a converted HAS2. The chief visual differences between the earlier marks and the updated ASW Sea King are the larger dorsal radome, with its flat top, and the array of blade aerials below the tactical compartment.
Westland Helicopters Ltd

Below: Evolved in 1982 to meet the need for a restored Royal Navy airborne early warning capability was the AEW version of the Sea King, which is fitted with a Thorn-EMI Searchwater surveillance radar in the starboard side-mounted radome. The radome swivels rearwards for stowage alongside the fuselage when the aircraft is off-task.
Westland Helicopters Ltd

Colour cameo: 8

The Mustang marque

Overleaf: A pair of P-51D Mustangs representing the many examples of the famous WW2 fighter kept in splendid airworthy condition on either side of the Atlantic. The left hand photo shows the appropriately registered N51JC, named *Cottonmouth*, at Harlingen, Tx during the Confederate Air Force's *Airsho 79* display.
Richard Odell

The picture on the right is of Stephen Grey's P-51D Mustang at the Biggin Hill International Air-Fair in May 1981. The aircraft is painted in an olive drab finish with the markings of the 362nd Fighter Squadron/357th Fighter Group of the USAAF's Eighth Air Force based at Leiston, Suffolk, in June 1944. The P-51D carries the name *Candyman* on the starboard side and the name *Moose* on the port side – the latter in reference to Lt Myron 'Moose' Becraft of the 362nd FS whose aircraft the Mustang is painted to represent. *Bob Warner*

Cottonmouth
CJ
J
N51JC
U.S. AIR FORCE

CANDYMAN
221

Colour cameo: 9 Lockheed TriStar

Left: The first Lockheed L-1011 TriStar, registered N1011, lifts-off from Palmdale, Ca on 16 November 1970 at the start of its 2hr 24min maiden flight. The first TriStar was fitted with Rolls-Royce RB211-22 turbofan engines derated to give a maximum thrust of 36,000lb, but it was later engaged in a succession of trials including the testing of higher thrust versions of the RB211 for subsequent models of the L-1011. The widebody Lockheed tri-jet entered service with Eastern Air Lines in the US on 26 April 1972. *Lockheed Corp*

Top: Purchases of the Lockheed tri-jet by Gulf Air, the Bahrain-headquartered airline, brought the number of TriStar customers into double figures. This photo shows the aircraft which was initially registered G-BDCW and later A40-TW, an L-1011-100. The 'Dash 100' version of the airliner is externally similar to the initial, medium-range, L-1011-1 variant of the TriStar but is cleared to operate at higher gross weights. *Lockheed Corp*

Above: A view of the TriStar flightline at Lockheed's Palmdale, Ca flight test and assembly plant in February 1974. In the foreground was the first TriStar for All Nippon Airways, JA8501, while the line-up to the rear included five TriStars for Eastern Air Lines, two for Delta and three for Air Canada. *Lockheed Corp*

The first srs 500 version of the L-1011 TriStar for Pan American World Airways, N501PA *Clipper Eagle*, operating out of Edwards AFB, Ca in early-1980 during pre-delivery flight trials. The 'Dash 500' is the long-range variant of the TriStar powered by three Rolls-Royce RB211-524B turbofans of 50,000lb thrust. This model of the L-1011 has a 13ft 6in – shorter fuselage, but trades reduced seating accommodation for increased fuel capacity and enhanced range. Notable among the recognition features of the – 500 is the extra fairing forward of the intake on the centre engine.

Top left: This threequarter rear view of a British Airways L-1011-1 TriStar, G-BBAF, at London Heathrow Airport conveys a good impression of the positioning of the centre engine in the aircraft's tailcone at the end of an S-shaped duct from the intake forward of the fin. *British Airports Authority*

Centre left: Two TriStars of the Saudi Arabian flag carrier, Saudia, at London Heathrow Airport in June 1976. Supplied as L-1011-100s, the aircraft were later modified to the L-1011-200 standard by being refitted with 48,000lb thrust RB211-524 engines, the extra power conferring improved ability to operate the airliner from 'hot or high' airports. *Saudia*

Below: An L-1011-100 of Trans World Airlines arriving at London Heathrow Airport on the carrier's Trans-Atlantic TriStar inaugural on 1 May 1978. The 'Dash 100' TriStar is a higher gross weight, increased fuel capacity version of the L-1011-1, for which the engine options included the uprated RB211-22F of 43,500lb thrust. *Lockheed Corp*

The noble 'Nine-Ack' -mainstay of the early RAF

R. A. Nicholls

Right: A late-production DH4, with an Eagle VIII engine, and showing the distance between the cockpits. The aircraft, A7995, was pictured without the Scarff ring gun-mounting. *British Aerospace, Hatfield*

Below: The first production DH9, C6051. Powered by a Siddeley Puma engine, the aircraft was tested at Martlesham Heath in November 1917 – with disappointing results. *British Aerospace, Hatfield*

THE only surviving Airco DH9A, a two-seat single-engined day bomber widely used by the RAF during its formative years, can now be seen in the Bomber Command Museum, Hendon, following extensive restoration. This is a most welcome and important addition to the collection at Hendon, for no aircraft did more to cement the foundations of the RAF than the DH9A. However, like the Lancaster of World War 2, the DH9A was in fact a successful redesign of a failure.

From March 1917 the pre-eminent British day bomber was the DH4, a Geoffrey de Havilland design produced by the Aircraft Manufacturing Company Ltd (Airco) and numerous sub-contractors. Serving extensively with the RNAS, RFC, and RAF in all theatres, the DH4 was demonstrably the best day bomber on either side during World War 1. Initially powered by the 230hp Beardmore-Halford-Pullinger (BHP) engine, the DH4 progressed by way of several more powerful alternatives to its ultimate powerplant, the 375hp Rolls-Royce Eagle VIII – in its Eagle VIII-powered version the DH4 was superb, with a turn of speed superior to contemporary scouts. The type's Achilles' heel was the cockpit layout, the pilot being under the centre-section and separated from the observer by the pressurised main fuel tank; speaking tubes, where fitted, were of little use in combat and communication was difficult, severely restricting the crews' fighting efficiency.

In mid-1917 German daylight raids on London led to demands for retaliatory action, and steps were taken to virtually double the RNAS/RFC bomber strength in order to carry the war deep into Germany itself. Excellent though the DH4 was, the design did not lend itself to the mass production which was essential if enough aircraft were to be built without delay, and it was therefore decided to modify the type to give both faster production and extended range. The result was the DH9, which first flew in late-1917 and was placed in production with a haste bordering on impetuosity, many outstanding DH4 orders being amended to specify DH9 even before the latter had been built in prototype form.

The DH9 was contemporarily described as 'a DH4 which has been officially interfered with to make it suitable for mass production and the Puma engine', and the cynicism of that description detracts nothing from its accuracy! It was indeed better suited to mass production – peak output reached 36 aircraft per day – but its performance was markedly inferior to the DH4 which it was to replace. The DH9's poor performance stemmed from the selection of outdated and unreliable engines in lieu of the DH4's Eagle VIII; the prototype was powered by the now-obsolescent 230hp BHP, built by Galloway as the 'Adriatic', while most production machines used the Siddeley Puma. The Puma was in fact a lightweight and 'improved' version of the BHP, designed for mass production and making extensive use of aluminium alloys, but the end result was most unreliable and from a projected power output of 300hp it was derated to 230. In November 1917 Geoffrey de Havilland unofficially voiced his misgivings about the DH9 to Major-General H. M. Trenchard, GOC the RFC in France, but despite the latter's outspoken criticism the Air Board remained obstinately committed to the type, huge orders having already been placed regardless of the Puma's lack of development.

Although a few DH9s reached No 103 Squadron, RFC, in December 1917 the type was not blooded until 9 March 1918, when aircraft of No 6 Squadron, RNAS, raided St Pierre Cappelle. Strategic bombing required the aircraft to operate at high altitude, typically some 15,000ft, to limit the risks from AA artillery and enemy scouts, while holding a disciplined formation so as to concentrate their defensive fire. However, the DH9 had great difficulty in climbing with a warload, and those aircraft which did make it were often unable to hold station and either had to turn back or descend to a lower and more dangerous altitude. The story of the DH9 in France is a catalogue of aborted sorties, engine failures, and high loss rates, and the DH4, a superior aircraft in most respects, remained in front-line service alongside its 'successor' for the duration of the war. The DH9's one redeeming feature was that the front cockpit and main fuel tank had been transposed, improving contact and co-operation between pilot and observer; but for this, the type's losses would undoubtedly have been even worse. Despite its shortcomings the DH9 served in large numbers and played a major part in bombing operations against Germany, but at a tragically high cost in both men and machines. That the DH9 achieved any measure of success was due to the courage and determination of the crews and the skill of the mechanics, not to any merit of the aircraft itself. Though it must be said in fairness that the DH9 fared better in less demanding theatres, and later played an important role in post-war civil aviation, in its primary employment as a Western Front day bomber it proved more of a liability than an asset.

The Air Board eventually listened to reason, and even as the DH9 entered service moves were afoot to redesign it around a more suitable engine. Airco were by now fully engaged on the design and development of the DH10 Amiens twin-engined bomber, and the project was therefore entrusted to Westland Aircraft Works of Yeovil, a company with previous experience of DH4 and DH9 production. Initial thinking favoured the Eagle VIII, but demand for that engine already far exceeded production – however, a promising alternative was available in the Liberty, a 400hp V-12 which the Packard Motor Co of America had just introduced.

Three prototypes of the redesigned aircraft, designated DH9A, were built by the conversion of DH9 airframes, the major modifications being strengthening of the forward fuselage to accomodate the Liberty and a substantial increase in wing span and chord. Delivery of the Liberty being somewhat delayed the first and second prototypes, B7664 and C6350, were fitted with Eagle VIIIs so that flight testing could proceed; both aircraft first flew in March 1918. The Liberty was available for installation in the third prototype, C6122, which first flew at Yeovil on 19 April in the hands of Capt A. R. Boeree and proved to be dangerously nose-heavy. This was corrected by increasing the wing stagger, and the top plane was re-rigged 2 inches further forward before C6122 flew up to Martlesham Heath for evaluation in May. All three prototypes showed a considerable improvement over the ill-starred DH9, particularly in service ceiling and rate of climb, but in neither of these respects did they match the Eagle VIII-powered DH4. The Liberty was adopted, 3,000 engines being ordered from Packard; orders were cut-back or cancelled after the Armistice, and considerably fewer than 3,000 were delivered. The DH9A's engine installation was 'cleaner' than that of the DH9, the Liberty being fully cowled and provided with a frontal radiator reminiscent of the DH4 – the DH9's engine was only partially cowled, the prominent exposed cylinder head and retractable underslung radiator bestowing a distinctly Germanic appearance. Quantity production was quickly under way, with new orders being placed and several existing DH9 orders switched to DH9A.

In armament the DH9A followed the general pattern of its predecessors though the bomb load, carried on

Below: The first prototype DH9A, B7664, with an Eagle VIII engine and four-bladed propeller; it was first flown by Capt B. C. Hucks in March 1918.
Westland Aircraft Ltd

bomb rails under the fuselage and lower mainplanes, was increased from 460 to 660lb. A single .303 Vickers machine gun, operated via a Bowden cable from a firing lever on the pilot's stick, was mounted on the port side of the fuselage and fired through the propeller disc by means of a Constantinesco hydraulic synchroniser. The observer was armed with a .303 Lewis gun on a Scarff No 2 ring mounting; twin Lewis guns on a double yoke could alternatively be mounted on the Scarff ring but this was seldom, if ever, done in practice.

Deliveries of DH9As to operational units began in June 1918, when Kenley-based No 110 Squadron received 18 examples. The Squadron's initial complement consisted of 'presentation' machines financed by His Serene Highness the Nizam of Hyderabad, for which reason the unit was henceforth titled No 110 (Hyderabad) Squadron. The worthy potentate's contribution to the war effort was further marked by an inscription on each aircraft – that this was permitted is somewhat surprising, since from 22 March 1918 it had been expressly forbidden for bomber aircraft to carry markings which might identify their squadron. On 31 August the Squadron moved overseas to Bettoncourt, France, as a unit of the Independent Force, RAF, but saw no action until 14 September. On that day 12 DH9As set out to bomb Boulay airfield; only six aircraft found the target, but all 12 returned safely. Between 14 September and 10 November the Squadron mounted a number of raids against German airfields and industrial targets, dropping 145 × 112lb and 33 × 230lb bombs. Three further Western Front squadrons, Nos 18, 99, and 205, converted to the DH9A but only No 18 completed the process before the Armistice. The type was quickly christened 'Nine-Ack', or 'Ninak', in RAF parlance, the name deriving from the first letter of the contemporary phonetic alphabet.

A total of 885 Nine-Acks had been built by the cessation of hostilities, of which roughly half had been delivered to the RAF in the UK and France. Although the type's brief wartime service spanned only 8 weeks of action its performance, once teething troubles with the Liberty's coil ignition were resolved, had fully matched Westland's expectations – had the war lasted into 1919 the DH9A would have completely replaced the DH4 and DH9 on the Western Front and spearheaded IF operations.

Wartime use of the DH9A was not restricted to the RAF; the type was used by No 2 Squadron, Canadian Air Force, and the US Marine Corps Northern Bombing Group received over 50 examples in September 1918, using them operationally in France during the final stages of the war. In addition, two Airco-built DH9As were shipped as pattern aircraft to the USA, where it was planned to build 4,000 'Americanised' examples as the USD-9 and USD-9A – despite the misleading designation of the former, both were DH9A derivatives. US construction was halted in 1919, but not before 13 such aircraft had been built, six by the Dayton-Wright Co of Dayton, Ohio, and seven by the Engineering Division of the US Army Bureau of Aircraft Production at McCook Field, Ohio. These aircraft were used in various McCook Field projects post-war, including pioneering work on pressurised cabins.

After the Armistice the Nine-Ack served briefly with the occupation forces in Germany, the carriage of

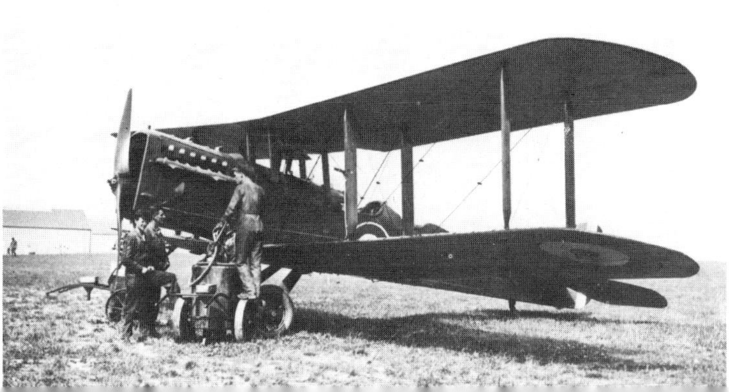

Above left: The third prototype DH9A, C6122, and the first to be fitted with the Liberty engine. *RAF Museum*

Left: An unarmed DH9A trainer, E797, of No 1 FTS Netheravon being serviced at its home base in 1921. *RAF Museum*

official mail being among the tasks undertaken; for this purpose some aircraft were fitted with a large mail pannier in place of the under-fuselage bomb rails. Between March and August 1919, DH9As of No 120 Squadron operated a cross-Channel mail service as part of the Aeroplane Postal Service, carrying official and private mail between the UK and Germany; the service was operated between Lympne or Hawkinge and Cologne, either direct or via France or Belgium. In late-1919 the RAE installed 450hp Napier Lion engines in 11 RAF DH9As, six of which were temporarily registered to HM Government as G-EAOF - EAOK; these were operated on the mail service by Aircraft Transport and Travel Ltd, an Airco subsidiary. The improved performance afforded by the Lion increased payload and enabled AT&T to maintain a reliable service across the Ardennes and Eifel throughout the winter of 1919-20, and the Company operated the mail run until mid-1920 when the DH9As returned to the RAF under their original serials.

The Russian Revolution and subsequent peace treaty between Soviet Russia and the Central Powers led to RAF units being sent to Russia to safeguard Allied interests and generally assist the White Russian forces attempting to stem the advance of Bolshevism. Among the units so engaged were Nos 47 and 221 Squadrons, operating mixed equipment including one flight each of DH9As; these DH9As saw intermittent action in Russia from mid-1919 until all RAF units were withdrawn in mid-1920, the Bolsheviks having won the day. Several DH9As fell into the hands of the Bolsheviks, who produced an exact copy which they called the R-1, powered by the M-5 engine, itself a Russian copy of the Liberty. The R-1 was operated in Russia until well into the 1930s, serving on wheel, ski, and float undercarriages, and 15 examples were supplied to Afghanistan in 1925.

With the drastic reduction in size of the RAF from its wartime peak to a much reduced peacetime establishment, the DH9A was selected to remain the standard light day bomber. Production continued, albeit on a far smaller scale, and contracts were awarded to Westlands and the newly-formed de Havilland Aircraft Co for the overhaul and reconditioning of large numbers of existing DH9A airframes. A great many reconditioned DH9As returned to service under new serials, making it difficult to determine true production figures with any accuracy.

Among the units to operate DH9As post-war was No 3 Squadron, re-formed at Leuchars in 1921 for fleet spotting and reconnaissance duties. Twelve DH9As were modified to 3-seat configuration for the Squadron's use pending issue of the Westland Walrus, a DH9A derivative developed for service with the fleet. The prototype, J6585, was converted from a standard DH9A as the Armstrong Whitworth Tadpole and retained the Liberty engine, but the 36 Westland-built production Walruses, N9500-9535, used the 450hp Napier Lion II. Despite detachable unstaggered wings, horn-balanced ailerons, third cockpit, and ventral prone compartment for the observer, the Walrus clearly showed its parentage, though it had now acquired the ungainly appearance which characterised fleet spotters of the 1920s. Designed for carrier operation the Walrus was equipped with arrester hooks, hydrovane, flotation bags, and a jettisonable oleo undercarriage, such nautical accessories being *de rigeur* for naval operations. The Walrus entered service with No 3 Squadron in early-1922, superseding the DH9A 3-seaters completely by the following October. The Squadron disbanded on 1 April 1923, its duties and aircraft being taken over by Fleet Spotter Flights. The Walrus proved unsuccessful and served only three years before being replaced by the Blackburn Blackburn and Avro Bison, but it is noteworthy as the first of several designs to make use of the large surplus stocks of DH9A components, stocks which parsimonious officialdom wanted to see put to practical use.

The outbreak of the Third Afghan War on India's NW Frontier in 1919 heralded the debut of the Nine-Ack in what would become its best-known role, as one of a succession of 'General Purpose' aircraft used by the RAF during the inter-war years. Together with Nos 48 (Bristol F2B) and 97 (DH10) Squadrons, No 99's DH9As were hastily dispatched from Germany to India to reinforce the small resident RAF presence. Based first at Ambala and later at Mianwali, the DH9As went into action against the Pathan tribesmen, supporting the garrison army units in the struggle to contain and repel the incursions of these fanatical fighting men. In 1920 the 'new' squadrons were renumbered, Nos 48, 97, and 99 becoming Nos 5, 60, and 27 Squadrons respectively.

None of the types used in India was ideal for such a climate, and performance suffered considerably; the fitment of tropical radiators from mid-1920 corrected matters somewhat, but even with this refinement the DH9A's service ceiling was reduced to 13,500ft. Nor was performance exactly enhanced by the wide range of supplementary equipment carried in deference to the hostile nature of the terrain over which the aircraft operated – a forced landing in the barren and mountainous NW Frontier region presented crews with the harsh prospect of attempting to survive in a desolate environment, while evading capture by an

Right: A nautical 'Nine-Ack' – N9523 was one of the 36 Westland Walrus fleet spotters. Oil spray from the Lion engine rendered the prone observer's compartment unusable for much of the time. *RAF Museum*

Below right: 'A' Flight, No 27 Squadron lined up on an airfield in India, circa 1924. *RAF Museum*

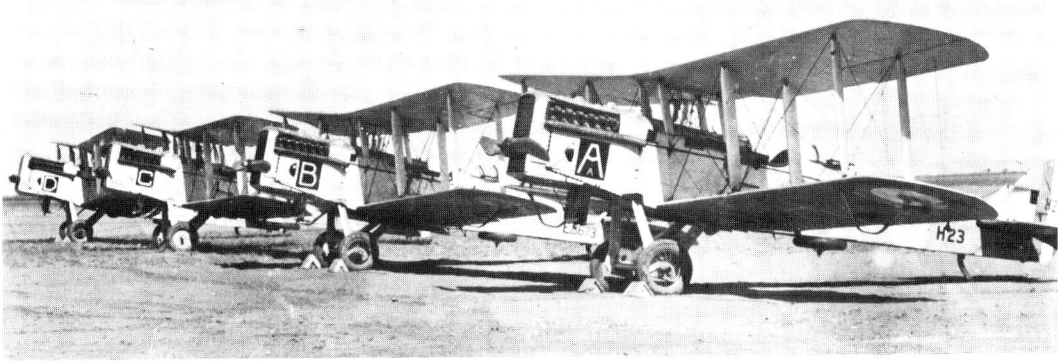

enemy whose treatment of prisoners was, to say the least, barbaric. The Nine-Acks were therefore burdened with such diverse impedimenta as; an auxiliary fuel tank, raising the endurance to 7hr; a spare wheel in case of punctures when landing away from base; food rations for three days; a supply of drinking water in goatskin bags; crew members' personal kit and bedding rolls; and a supply of bottled beer, this last item presumably ensuring that one's spirits did not flag! Given that these items were additional to the required operational load, one can see why the Nine-Ack is reputed to have introduced the phrase 'everything but the kitchen sink' into RAF usage!

The RAF's India Group was the poor relation in a service which was grossly under-funded as a whole, and carried out a difficult task in primitive conditions, starved of money, equipment, spares, and facilities. Consequently serviceability rates were low, cannibalisation commonplace, and the appearance of aircraft generally well-worn. The scandalous conditions in India led to AVM Sir John Salmond being sent out in 1922 to make an on-the-spot investigation and report on the causes of the Group's low efficiency. Salmond's report, presented to the Viceroy of India in October 1922, made numerous recommendations for the improved financing, administration, and operational employment of the India Group; the report was accepted and the implementation of its recommendations, though painfully slow, did result in a gradual improvement in the position of the RAF in India.

In 1923 No 60 Squadron's DH10s were replaced by the more suitable DH9A and this unit, together with No 27 Squadron, continued to operate the type from various Indian bases for a further seven years. During their service in India the DH9A squadrons were on an almost continual operational footing, undertaking the near-impossible task of peacekeeping in an area where the populace alternated between the twin pursuits of dividing in inter-tribal conflict and uniting in rebellion against the British Raj.

The DH9A's activities in India were not exclusively belligerent in nature, but included several pioneering long-distance flights. One such venture in January 1925 saw all six Flight Commanders of Nos 27 and 60 Squadrons setting out to fly the 1,330 miles from Risalpur to Calcutta, a journey eventually completed in 14½ hr flying spread over four days. A further task was that of casualty evacuation, the patient being strapped into a Neil Robertson stretcher secured to the top of the rear fuselage; this method was used to transfer serious cases from the forward area to base hospital, thus avoiding a long and arduous overland journey which the casualty was in no condition to make.

Between December 1928 and February 1929 the DH9As took part in an extended mercy mission when the RAF responded to an urgent call from the British Legation in Kabul for the swift evacuation of foreign nationals from the city. Kabul was surrounded by rebels attempting to overthrow King Amanullah, the Afghan ruler; the situation was grave and the only way into or out of the city was by air. Loyal forces secured the city, including Sherpur airstrip, and Vickers Victorias of No 70 Squadron and DH9As of Nos 27 and 60 Squadrons began airlifting the civilians and their belongings to India, operating through the worst winter in living memory. The airlift was completed on 25 February 1929, 586 civilians and 24,193lb of baggage having been brought out of the beleaguered city without any loss of life. Thus ended the first mass airlift of civilians, achieved under difficult conditions for the loss of only two aircraft, a DH9A brought down by rifle fire and a Victoria which was abandoned after a forced landing.

Defence spending was minimal in the 1920s and the DH9A had to soldier on long after it was due for replacement – that it did so, and continued to be effective, speaks volumes for the ruggedness and reliability of both airframe and engine. Its days in India came to an end in 1930 when Nos 27 and 60 Squadrons re-equipped with the Westland Wapiti IIA, another aircraft designed to make the maximum possible use of DH9A components.

The British Protectorate of Egypt, strategically placed astride the Suez Canal, was both a convenient stepping-stone en route to British possessions in Africa and 'East of Suez' and a central base among the turbulent Arab states. It was thus an ideal hub for post-war RAF operations overseas, with an establishment of seven squadrons plus a depot and flying and gunnery schools. DH9As served in Egypt with No 4 FTS at Abu Sueir and with Nos 8 (1920-21), 45 (1927-29), and 47 (1920-27) Squadrons.

The dismemberment of the Ottoman Empire after World War 1 freed vast areas of the Middle East from Turkish rule. These unstable and undeveloped areas were divided into states by the League of Nations, each state being placed under the supervision of either France or Britain. France assumed the mandate for Syria, while Iraq (formerly Mesopotamia), Palestine, and Transjordan came under Britain. The mandate holder was responsible for the state's defence, internal security, and development towards eventual independence. Of the states under British mandate Iraq was the largest and most difficult to administer, the required military presence being assessed as six

Right: A No 27 Squadron crew with an improbable combination of clothing, to cater for the extreme temperature variations between ground level and operational altitude. *RAF Museum*

Far right: DH9A, E873, of No 84 Squadron airborne from Shaibah, Iraq, and carrying tropical radiator, auxiliary fuel tank, and spare wheel. Note wingtip and tail navigation lights fitted. *British Aerospace, Hatfield*

cavalry battalions, 33 infantry battalions, and 16 batteries of artillery. The newly-created states were not recognised by Turkey, nor was the mandate universally welcomed by the Iraqis, many of whom felt that they had simply exchanged Turkish domination for British, and a widespread revolt in 1919-20 was only put down at a cost of 876 British troops killed. Stability in Iraq was threatened by insurrection, both native and Turkish inspired, together with Turkish incursions across the common border in the north. The sheer scale and cost of the problem led Trenchard, now Chief of the Air Staff, to propose a bold plan whereby responsibility for policing Iraq would be transferred from the army to the RAF, a policy of 'air control'. This plan was accepted and on 1 October 1922 RAF Iraq Command assumed military control of Iraq, a venture which many expected to end in abject failure. From the vast army presence forces were reduced to a single Anglo-Indian infantry brigade supporting an RAF establishment of eight squadrons of aircraft and four of RAF-manned armoured cars. The aircraft element consisted of four DH9A squadrons (Nos 8 and 30 at Hinaidi, No 55 at Mosul, and No 84 at Shaibah); one Sopwith Snipe squadron (No 1 at Hinaidi); one Bristol F2B squadron (No 6 at Kirkuk); and two Vickers Vernon troop carrier squadrons (Nos 45 and 70 at Hinaidi). Clearly the bulk of any bombing, reconnaissance, and close-support operations would fall to the Nine-Acks.

Many well-intentioned voices were raised in protest at the supposedly inhuman use of air control against rebel tribesmen, mainly by public figures in Britain with no appreciation of the task. In fact, even the briefest study shows that air control achieved its ends with greater flexibility, lower loss of life, and at a far lower cost than was possible with ground troops. The Nine-Acks were used primarily on offensive operations against rebel tribesmen and infiltrating Turkish troops, but also undertook supply dropping and casualty evacuation. Aircraft were lost to rebel small-arms fire, but such was the nature of the sparsely populated terrain that on a number of occasions a 'downed' aircraft was located in hostile territory, repaired by a ground party flown in by Vernon, and flown back to base. As in India, such eventualities were catered for by carrying the approved range of emergency equipment in and on the aircraft. Despite almost continuous operations in Iraq, much peaceful work was also carried out, including the aerial survey and mapping of the entire southern half of the country. Wapitis began replacing DH9As in Iraq in 1928, though No 55 Squadron did not begin re-equipping until 1930, relinquishing its last Nine-Acks in February 1931.

Successful use of air control in Iraq led to its adoption in Transjordan and the Aden Protectorate, the DH9A serving in both areas. The type also saw service in the Sudan and Turkey, DH9A units twice being sent to the latter country when Turkish Nationalist ambitions in the Dardenelles, coupled with Turkish-Greek tension, threatened the fragile stability of the region.

Although the majority of the Nine-Acks used in the Middle East and India were of standard configuration,

Top: DH9As of the Hinaidi-based No 55 Squadron in formation over Iraq, circa 1927. *RAF Museum*

Above: Two DH9As of No 14 Squadron, which operated in Palestine and Transjordan, based at Ramleh and Amman. Note the fitment of Handley Page slots. *RAF Museum*

several were converted locally to carry a rear seat passenger in lieu of the gunner. With all armament removed, these examples served as communications hacks and as personal transports for senior RAF commanders, the latter being dubbed 'Racing Red Nines' owing to their distinctive finish of blood-red overall with white struts.

While the Nine-Ack is best remembered for its activities in hotter climes, it also saw widespread service with home-based units. Twelve aircraft from the first Airco production batch were taken on Royal Navy charge in August 1918; these were almost certainly the aircraft which, although on RN charge, were operated for a short period by Nos 212 and 273 Squadrons, RAF. Based at Great Yarmouth, both units operated mixed equipment including DH9As, which were used for coastal reconnaissance and anti-submarine patrols off the East Coast.

Another unit to number DH9As among its mixed equipment was No 24 Squadron, which re-formed at Kenley on 1 February 1920 as a communications and training squadron. No 24's primary role was that of providing a high-speed courier service for senior officers and government officials, with the secondary task of making aircraft available for the 'refresher' training of pilots temporarily grounded by a posting to the Air Ministry. To these ends the Squadron operated a mixed complement of converted Bristol F2Bs and DH9As, together with a Flight of Avro 504 trainers. The DH9As remained with the Squadron when it moved to Northolt in January 1927, and were replaced by Wapitis and Fairey IIIFs in June of that year. Between 1924 and 1926 the type also served in an experimental role with No 15 Squadron, which re-formed in March 1924 as a bombing and ballistics trials unit, attached to the Aeroplane and Armament Experimental Establishment (A&AEE) at Martlesham Heath.

Several home-based squadrons operated DH9As briefly before re-equipping with more modern types, but only Nos 39 and 207 flew them in the light bomber role for an extended period. Both squadrons became well known through their formation flying displays and demonstrations of precision 'bombing' which regularly thrilled the crowds at the Hendon RAF Pageants and Displays in the 1920s. No 207 Squadron also served as the guinea pig for numerous trial installations, including use of early R/T equipment and tests of RAE designed engine silencers.

Though rapidly approaching obsolescence, the Nine-Ack enjoyed a new lease of life in the mid-1920s as the mount of Nos 600, 601, 602, 603, and 605 Squadrons of the newly-formed Auxiliary Air Force (AAF). In the hands of the 'weekend fliers' the

Below: 'Nine-Acks' of No 39 Squadron based at Spitalgate, Grantham, practising for the 1927 Hendon Air Display. Note the non-standard radiator cap on J7073, nearest the camera. *British Aerospace Hatfield*

Above: Aircraft of No 601 (County of London) Squadron, Auxiliary Air Force, in the Squadron's hangar at Hendon, circa August 1930. Two DH9As were pictured plus two Wapitis, with which the Squadron was progressively re-equipping. *RAF Museum*

Nine-Ack received further acclaim through participation in the RAF Displays and the Air Defence Exercises, in which 'Redland' annually engaged 'Blueland' to test the Air Defences of Great Britain. The AAF Nine-Acks eventually gave way to Fairey Fawns and Westland Wapitis, and by late-1930 the type had disappeared from first-line UK service.

In 1926 de Havillands produced the ultimate Nine-Ack development, the Bristol Jupiter-powered DH9AJ Stag. With increased wing area, the Jupiter engine, and an oleo undercarriage, the Stag offered improved performance over the Liberty-powered DH9A and was among the types entered for assessment under AM Spec.26/27 for a Nine-Ack replacement. Following tests at Martlesham Heath the production contract was awarded to the Westland Wapiti, and DH9AJ production never went beyond the single prototype, J7028.

A total of some 2,140 Nine-Acks had been built when production ceased after the delivery of a final batch of 35 dual-control trainer versions in 1927. The re-equipment of No 55 Squadron at Hinaidi in 1931 marked the end of the DH9A in RAF squadron service; numerous other examples served in the training and communications roles at home and overseas, while still others were engaged on experimental work and trials with the RAE and various manufacturers.

Extended RAF service meant that few DH9As appeared on civil registers. Six aircraft powered variously by Eagle, Liberty, and Lion engines, were registered to the Aircraft Disposal Co Ltd for racing and demonstration use, while the temporary registration of the Lion-powered mail-planes has already been mentioned. DH9As were presented to Australia and Canada as part of the 1920 Imperial Gift; the 29 Australian machines remained in storage until entering RAAF service in 1925, while the 11 given to Canada were immediately registered to the Canadian Air Board Civil Operations Branch and allotted to forestry patrol, aerial survey, and mail carrying duties.

In the civil context the DH9R and DH16 merit brief mention. The single DH9R, G-EAHT, was a Nine-Ack-based Lion-powered sesquiplane racer. Registered to AT & T in 1919, the single-seat DH9R won several races and broke a number of speed records before being scrapped in 1922. The DH16 was built for AT & T's London-Paris route and used DH9A components, though the rear fuselage was modified to provide an enclosed four-place cabin. Six Eagle and three Lion-powered DH16s were built by Airco and all nine were registered to AT & T; the type enjoyed a brief commercial life with that company, and one example was resold to the River Plate Aviation Co of Buenos Aires in April 1920.

Today only one Nine-Ack survives and that is the exquisite example which now stands in the Bomber Command Museum, contrasting dramatically with the Wellington, Lancaster, Valiant, and Vulcan of later generations. The survivor is F1010, c/no WA8459AMA, a Westland-built aircraft issued to No 110 Squadron and taken to France on 31 August 1918. F1010 was the Squadron's 13th aircraft, but for superstitious reasons was inscribed 'Hyderabad No 12A'. This machine had flown 25hr and completed five missions when it was brought down during a raid on

Left: J7028, the sole example of the Jupiter-powered DH9AJ Stag. Originally intended for the Napier Lion engine, it was never built in that form. *RAF Museum*

Below: One of the three Lion-powered DH16s seen coupled to a Hucks starter at the 1920 Olympia Aero Show. Note the enclosed four-place cabin. *British Aerospace, Hatfield*

Kaizerslautern on 5 October, the pilot and observer, Capt A.G. Inglis and 2-Lt W.C.L. Bodley, being unharmed and taken prisoner. Virtually intact, F1010 was removed to Berlin, where it remained in the Berlin Air Museum until 1943, at which time the Museum's contents were removed to Krakow for safety during the Allied bombing of the German capital. During the journey the truck carrying F1010's wings and tailplane is believed to have gone astray, never to be seen again; the circumstances may be open to question, but the items were indeed lost, and F1010 spent the next 34 years in a semi-derelict condition in the Polish Aviation and Astronautics Museum in Krakow. In 1968 moves were initiated to acquire F1010 for the (then) projected RAF Museum, and negotiations finally bore fruit in 1977 when the Polish authorities agreed to exchange the aircraft for a Spitfire XV. F1010 was delivered to the RAF Museum's Cardington workshop in June 1977, since when the construction of new mainplanes and tail surfaces has proceeded slowly but surely, subject to priority on other projects. Five years of painstaking work by the RAF Museum's small band of dedicated tradesmen, under the able and skilled direction of the unit's Keeper, M.P. (Bill) Sayer, brought F1010 to completion at the end of 1982 and it now appears exactly as it did on 5 October 1918 when Inglis and Bodley took off from Bettoncourt on its final operation.

The Nine-Ack arrived too late to play a significant part in World War 1, and is generally thought of as having been basically a peace-time aircraft – in reality its career spanned 13 years during which the RAF was almost continuously engaged in operations in overseas theatres. The Nine-Ack played a leading role in these operations, proving a stalwart and reliable workhorse in all its various guises and earning for itself a place of honour in the history of the RAF.

Below: The RAF Museum's 'Nine-Ack', F1010, in the final stages of restoration in early-1983. At first glance the fuselage may appear little different from the time of its arrival from Krakow, but in fact the structure has been almost completely rebuilt. The plywood covering of the forward fuselage is clearly seen here. *R. A. Nicholls*

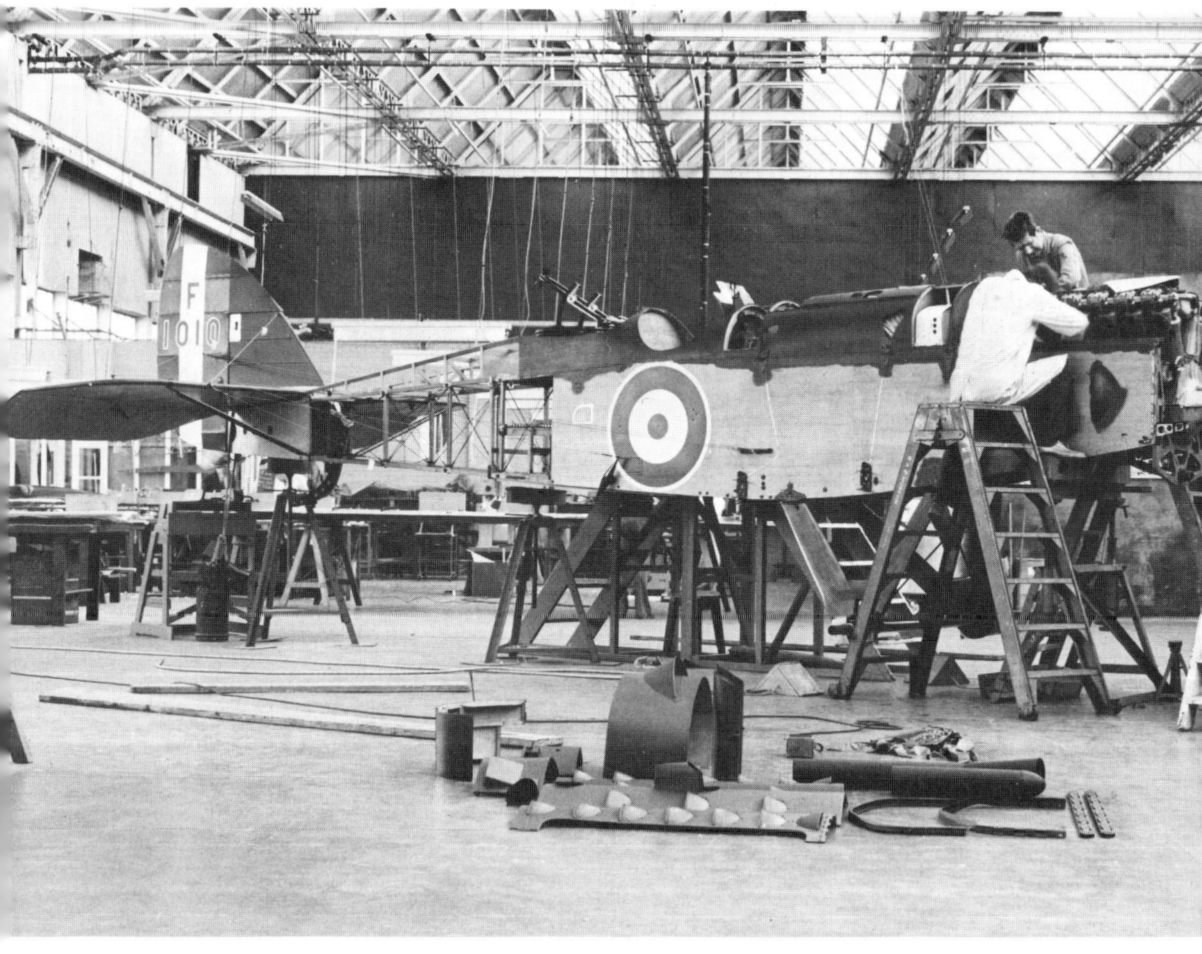

Left: View of a DH9A's pilot's panel to 1918 standard, as seen on F1010. Note the bead of the ring and bead gunsight (left), and the rear support for the Aldis tube sight, which had still to be fitted. *R. A. Nicholls*

Comparative data and performance figures – DH4, DH9, and DH9A.

	DH4	DH9	DH9A
Powerplant	375hp R-R Eagle VIII	230hp Siddeley Puma	400hp Liberty 12
Wingspan	42ft 4⅝ in	42ft 4⅝ in	45ft 10¾in
Wing area	434 ft^2	434 ft^2	486¾ ft^2
Chord	5ft 6in	5ft 6in	5ft 9in
Length	30ft	30ft 5in	30ft 3in
Height	11ft	11ft 2in	11ft 4in
Tailspan	14ft	14ft	14ft
Empty weight	2,387lb	2,203lb	2,800lb
Loaded weight	3,472lb*	3,669lb	4,645lb
Max speed at Sea Level	143 mph*	–	123 mph
Max speed at 10,000ft	133.5 mph*	111.5 mph	114.5 mph
Max speed at 15,000ft	126 mph*	97.5 mph	106 mph
Initial climb	1,350ft/min*	625ft/min	890ft/min
Time to 10,000ft	9min*	20min 5sec	15min 35sec
Time to 15,000 ft	16min 30sec*	45min	33min
Ceiling	23,500ft*	15,500ft	16,750ft
Endurance (normal)	3¾ hr	4½ hr	5¼ hr
Armament	1 × .303 Vickers 1 × .303 Lewis 460lb bomb load	1 × .303 Vickers 1 × .303 Lewis 460lb bomb load	1 × .303 Vickers 1 × .303 Lewis 660lb bomb load

Note
*Figures relate to aircraft without bomb load (DH4).
DH9 and DH9A figures refer to aircraft with bombs.

The DH9A in RAF Squadron service, 1918–1931.

Sqn	Service Period	France/ Germany	Russia	UK	Aden	Egypt	India	Iraq	Palestine + T Jordan	Sudan	Turkey
3	921–22			*							
8	920–28				*	*		*			
11	923–24			*							
12	923–24			*							
14	924–29								*		
15	924–26			*							
18	918–19	*									
24	920–27			*p							
25	918–19	*p									
27	920–30						*				
30	921–29							*			
35	929–30			*							
39	923–28			*							
45	927–29					*					
47	919–28		*p			*				*	
55	920–31							*			*
57	919	*									
60	923–30						*				
84	920–28							*			
99	918–20	*					*				
100	1922–24			*p							
101	1928–29			*							
110	1918–19	*									
120	1918–19			*							
205	1918–19	*									
207	1920–27			*							*
212	1918–20			*p							
221	1918–19		*p								
273	1918–19			*p							
501	1930			*							
600	1925–29			*							
601	1926–30			*							
602	1925–28			*							
603	1925–30			*							
604	1930			*							
605	1926–30			*							

(i) 'p' indicates unit partially equipped with DH9A.
(ii) No 99 Squadron was renumbered No 27 at Mianwali, India on 1.4.20.
(iii) No 47 Squadron became 'A' Squadron, RAF Mission, 7.10.19.
No 206 Squadron was renumbered No 47 at Helwan, Egypt, on 1.2.20 and received DH9As the following year.

Acknowledgement
The author would like to record his appreciation of the generous provision of contemporary photographs by the credited sources.

US National Air and Space Museum

Peter Clifton

ON Independence Avenue, Washington DC, the National Air and Space Museum provides an elegant and substantial home for the cream of US aviation museum collections – and not just of aviation, for the exhibits range from the original Wright Flyer to examples of the Gemini and Apollo spacecraft. Opened in 1976, the US Bicentennial Year, the completion of the Museum represented the fulfilment of a $40 million programme by the Smithsonian Institution to accommodate its priceless assembly of aerospace artefacts. Among the most memorable of these – in addition to the Flyer with which Wilbur and Orville Wright ushered in the era of manned and powered flight at Kitty Hawk, NC on 17 December 1903 – are the Ryan monoplane flown by Capt Charles Lindbergh on the first non-stop solo flight across the Atlantic on 20-21 May 1927, and the Apollo 11 command module that featured in the epoch-making lunar landing mission of 16-24 July 1969.

The Museum displays are presented in a series of Halls each given over to certain aerospace themes. The exhibits already mentioned are located appropriately in the Milestones of Flight Hall. Other Halls are devoted to Air Transport, World War 1 and World War 2 aircraft, Vertical Flight, Flight Technology, and Space Flight. Additional areas of the complex are set aside for general aviation exhibits, balloon gondolas, and air traffic control.

Many of the displays are presented in imaginative settings; for example, there is a Sea-Air Operations Gallery which is arranged in part to appear as the hangar deck of an aircraft carrier; and the World War 1 exhibition makes use of a Western Front airfield diorama. The exhibits include numerous aircraft models and paintings, among the latter being a giant size Keith Ferris mural of a B-17 Flying Fortress mission.

The Museum, large as it is, far from houses the entire aircraft collection of the Smithsonian, the remainder of which is stored at Silver Hill, Md. However, the exhibits at the Museum are periodically exchanged with those in storage at Silver Hill, so even recurrent visits to the National Air and Space Museum are likely to be rewarded with new sights of America's aviation heritage.

Top: Exhibits in the Hall of Air Transportation include a Ford Tri-Motor (rear fuselage, top of photo); a Douglas DC-3, N18124 (c/n 2000), in the markings of Eastern Air Lines – the aircraft was delivered to the airline on 7 December 1937 and donated to the Smithsonian in May 1953; and a Boeing 247D, this aircraft came third in the 1934 London-Melbourne race. *All photos: Peter Clifton*

Above: The Milestones of Flight Gallery has Lindbergh's *Spirit of St Louis* prominently displayed.

Right: The Bell X1A, 46-062 *Glamorous Glennis*, the first piloted aircraft to exceed the speed of sound after dropping from the belly of a B-29 in October 1947.

Far right, top: A Lockheed F-104, N818NA, in NASA markings and not long retired from flight test operations at Edwards AFB, Ca.

Far right, centre: The Northrop M2 F3 lifting body designed to operate at the wide range of speeds that the Space Shuttle orbiter demands.

Far right, bottom: Inside the Sea-Air Operations gallery, simulating an aircraft carrier hangar deck, and displaying a variety of naval aircraft from the Boeing F4B-4 to the Douglas A-4C Skyhawk; in the centre of this picture is a Douglas SBD-6 Dauntless.

NASA
818
N818NA

GLAMOROUS
GLENNIS

NASA
803
FLIGHT RESEARCH CENTER
CCCP

109
E10

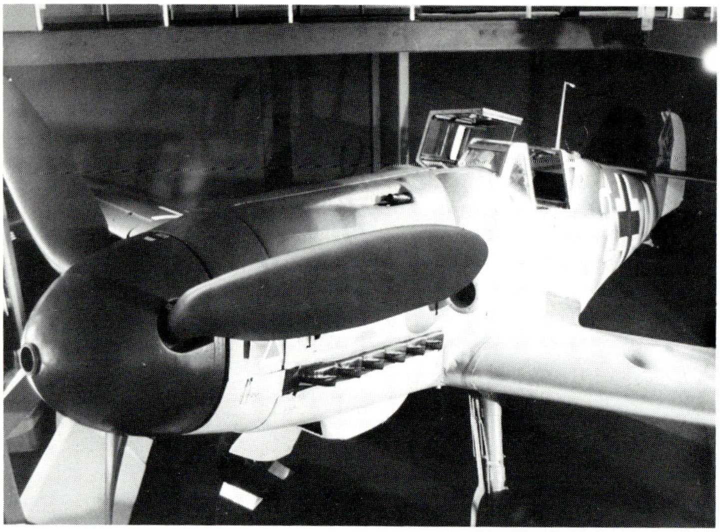

Top: Classic WW2 fighters in the Museum include a Messerschmitt Bf109G6 and . . .

Above: . . . Macchi 202 with P-51 Mustang below it. Just visible in the background is part of the Flying Fortress mission mural.

Right: Another look at part of the Air Transport Hall with a Northrop Alpha, NC11Y, in TWA markings.

PITCAIRN
MAILWING
21
U.S. MAIL
NORTHROP
ALPHA

History of the 8° Stormo

A. Palma

THE history of the *8° Stormo* of the present day Italian Air Force, the *Aeronautica Militare Italiana (AMI)*, encompasses in addition to its service as a fighter-bomber wing from 1967 to date, a span of 14 years' operations from 1927 – 1929 and 1931 – 1943 as a component of the earlier Italian Air force, the *Regia Aeronautica (RA)*, of the inter-war and WW2 era. As might be imagined the recent history of the *8° Stormo* has proved to be a much more settled period than that experienced by the wing in the 1930s and 40s, when operations were characterised by numerous changes in equipment and bases – as far afield as Spain and East Africa. Since 1971 the *Stormo* has been flying Fiat G91Ys, the twin-engined, multi-role derivative of the G-91R; and, accordingly, the unit's full designation for the past 12 years has been the *8° Stormo Caccia-Bombardieri-Ricognitori*, this label incorporating its multi-purpose fighter-bomber and reconnaissance mission.

The *8° Stormo* was founded as a night bomber wing at Ciampino Sud, Rome on 1 July 1927, the formation of the unit embodying the *Regia Aeronautica's* plans in developing a bomber force that would realise the air force strategies of Gen Giulio Douhet. The *Stormo* comprised two Groups – the *26° Gruppo* with the *11° and 13° Squadriglie* and the *86° Gruppo* which had assigned to it the *190°* and *191° Squadriglie* (the general pattern of organisation in flying units of the *RA* bore some comparison of that of the German *Luftwaffe*; the *Squadriglia*, or 'Squadron', amounted to nine aircraft and was the equivalent of a German *Staffel*, while up to three *Squadriglie* normally formed a *Gruppo*, or Group, and the two *Gruppi* then comprised a *Stormo*, or Wing).

The squadrons of the *26° Gruppo* were equipped with Caproni Ca73 biplane bombers whereas the *86° Gruppo* flew Macchi M24 seaplanes. In view of their diverse aircraft the *8° Stormo's* two Groups were based separately at Ciampino Sud and the seaplane station of Brindisi.

The following year, the composition of the Wing was complicated by the attachment of an autonomous Group at Ciampino Sud in the light ground-attack role, the *7° Gruppo* made up of four squadrons – the *76°, 84°, 86°, and 96° Squadriglie* – equipped with Ansaldo AC3s. This radial engined, parasol wing monoplane was a licence-built version of the French-designed Dewoitine D9, armed with two synchronised Vickers 7.62mm machine guns firing through the propeller arc and a 7.5mm machine gun angled upwards over the wing. As a result of the addition of the *7° Gruppo*, the *8° Stormo* became known as a 'Mixed Stormo'.

During this early period of its existence the 8th Wing conducted an intensive training programme that

Italian Air Force

often involved the technical trials of equipment and aircraft. The *26° Gruppo*, in particular, was concerned with long-range navigation and bombing training.

Further re-equipment took place in 1929 when the *7° Gruppo* received Fiat CR20 biplane fighters and the *86° Gruppo* took delivery of Savoia-Marchetti SM55 flying boats. The latter were the remarkble looking twin-hulled and tandem engined machines famous for their succession of long-range flights from 1927 onwards in the hands of pioneer Italian aviators. The *86° Gruppo* took part in the East Mediterranean Air Cruise directed by General Balbo on 5-19 June 1929, covering nearly 3,000 miles in the process.

For the *8° Stormo* itself, the year 1929 was less auspicious; in fact, the Wing-level organisation was disbanded in June of that year and its assigned *Gruppi* became autonomous units operating under command of the *3° Zona Aerea Territoriale.*

However, after an interval of only two years, the *8° Stormo* was re-formed, this time headquarted at Ferrara and comprising the *27° Gruppo* with the *17°* and *18° Squadriglie* plus the *28° Gruppo* with the *10°* and *19° Squadriglie*, both Groups operating variants of the Caproni Ca73 with the 27th located at Gorizia and the 28th based at Lonate Pozzolo. For some months the Stormo was kept on the move by successive changes of base; on 20 August the entire Wing moved into Gorizia but four days later decamped back to Ferrara to take part in the 1931 air manoeuvres. Finally, on 13

Above: G91Ys of the *8° Stormo* on the flightline at Cervia-San Giorgio AB. *Toselli and Grattoni Archives*

October, the Stormo took up residence at Poggio Renatico. During the ensuing months the Stormo took part in many exercises and air shows of national importance as well as conducting intensive training. New equipment continued to be taken on strength, including the Breda Ba15S and, from August 1934, Caproni Ca102, the latter being the twin Jupiter VII-powered version of the three-engined Ca101. The Wing's training paid off that year when the *27° Gruppo* won the 'Blue Ribbon Cup' over the Furbara range.

In October 1935, the *8° Stormo* was deployed to East Africa where it took part in the Abyssinian operation. The *27° Gruppo* operated with its *17° Squadriglia* from Massaua and the *18° Squadriglia* at Assab, while the Wing Headquarters was based at Gura. The *28° Gruppo* joined the rest of the Wing in December 1935. In that year a further re-equipment had taken place with the receipt of Caproni Ca111s; this was a single engined reconnaissance and support aircraft derived from the Ca101. The Wing's mission alternated bombing, reconnaissance and supply drop sorties in support of the Italian Army's campaign over the inhospitable terrain of Abyssinia.

Meanwhile, back in Italy, November 1935 had seen the establishment of a supplementary unit in the form

Right: A Caproni Ca74G of the *19° Squadriglia, 28° Gruppo,* at Lonate Pozzolo in the early-1930s. *Vigna's Archive*

Below: A Breda 15S belonging to the *2° Zona Aerea Territoriale.* Aircraft of this type began to join the *8° Stormo* in 1931. *Vigna's Archive*

of the *8° Stormo bis* at Poggio Renatico. The unit, thought to have been mainly tasked with the training of new aircrews for duty in East Africa, was equipped with a variety of aircraft – Ca74s, Ca100s, Ca102s and Ca111s – but in January 1936 it moved to Borgo Panigale near Bologna where it re-equipped with the much newer Savoia Marchetti SM81 *'Pipistrello'* (Bat), a tri-motor monoplane used on bomber or transport duties.

During the period in East Africa the *17° Squadriglia* of the *27° Gruppo* changed its designation number to the *52° Squadriglia* following a series of mishaps, including the loss of all its aircraft in a hangar explosion at Gura airfield on 25 December 1935. The new number for the squadron, 52, was derived from the addition of the 17, 8, and 27 numbers of the squadron, wing and group. Even today the superstition about the squadron's former number stemming from this incident is still apparent in the *AMI* with a general reluctance having been expressed on many occasions about using the figure 17 on unit designations or aircraft codes.

The *8° Stormo* returned to Italy on 20 July 1936 having suffered the loss of 15 aircrew personnnel and flown 5,060hr during the course of 2,431 sorties. Further combat operations in another war zone were less than a year away when, in January 1937, the Stormo re-equipped with Savoia Marchetti SM79 medium bombers, the aircraft known as the *'Sparviero'* or Hawk. After a difficult transition caused by technical problems with the SM79s and the transfer of experienced personnel (including 115 pilots) to other units, the *Stormo* completed its work-up and in November 1937 received orders to take part in operations in Spain in support of the Nationalist forces engaged in the Civil War.

From January 1938 both the *27°* and *28° Gruppi* were based at Palma de Mallorca. It was a presence kept as inconspicous as possible – the aircrews were all volunteers, they went to Spain under false names, and the aircraft markings were disguised. The involvement of the *8° Stormo* in the Spanish Civil War ended in May 1939 and the following month the aircraft and personnel returned to Italy, where the Wing was disbanded.

The absence of the *8° Stormo* from the *Regia Aeronautica's* first-line strength only lasted for a little over a month, however, as the unit was re-formed at Alghero on 1 July 1939, again equipped with SM79s. The composition of the Wing was as before, with the

Left: In 1935, equipped with Caproni Ca111s, the Wing took part in the Abyssinian campaign – one of the Ca111s is seen during a sortie from the base at Gura. *Vigna's Archive*

Below left: A Savoia Marchetti SM81'*Pipistrello*' tri-motor monoplane of the *19°* *Squadriglia* photographed near the unit's home base of Bologna-Borgo Panigale in 1936. *Italian AF*

18th and 52nd Squadrons forming the 27th Group and the 10th and 19th Squadrons in the 28th Group.

Some six weeks after the launch of the German *Blitzkrieg* on the Low Countries and France, Italy declared war on France and Great Britain, on 10 June 1940, and that day the *8° Stormo* moved to Villacidro in preparation for the coming conflict. The *Stormo* was one of three SM79-equipped *RA* Wings in Central Italy reporting to the *3ª Squadra Aerea* – the area command. The *8° Stormo's* first combat missions in WW2 were flown on 15 June 1940 against French bases in Corsica. The campaign against France was a short-lived one, Italy having entered the war at a late stage; and the fighting over Southern France, Corsica and Tunisia was followed by an Armistice on 19 June in the aftermath of France's cessation of hostilites with Germany. The *Stormo*'s attention then turned to the British naval forces in the Mediterranean, with attacks against Royal Navy ships and convoys in transit from Gibraltar to Malta and Egypt.

In September 1940 the *Stormo* moved to Alghero to regroup for reconnaissance duties and to conduct training of the new aircrews brought in to replace personnel lost during the opening months of the war. A deployment to Decimomannu in Sardinia was made at the end of November 1940 to conduct bombing operations against British naval forces off Cape Teulada, the Wing later returning to Italy and moving back to Villacidro.

In April 1941 the headquarters of the *8° Stormo* and the *27° Gruppo* relocated to Misurata in North Africa and then to Bengazi and Marturba, the *28° Gruppo* remaining at Villacidro until the end of May before moving to Misurata and then Martuba. For the remainder of 1941 the *Stormo* was continously engaged in the fighting in Libya as the Axis forces drove the British back towards Egypt. The *8° Stormo* took part in day and night bombing raids, reconnaissance and ground attack sorties, notably against the air bases at Tobruk and Mersa Matruh and Mediterranean convoys. In December the Wing was withdrawn to Barce and Misurata, and then back to Italy.

January 1942 saw the *8° Stormo* regrouping at Perugia for a renewed training period on the SM79s and a work-up on the newly received CRDA CANT Z1007 bis trimotor, twin-fin medium bombers. At this time the Wing was also training aircrew additional to its own complement, a task which was continued from Viterbo after yet another move on 23 June. After a

Left: This view of a Savoia Marchetti SM79 is of particular interest as it shows one of the *8° Stormo* aircraft flying near Palma de Mallorca while deployed there in 1938 to take part in the Spanish Civil War – note the Spanish markings on the aircraft. *Vigna's Archive*

Below left: An SM79 of the *19° Squadriglia* at Castel Benito in Libya during 1941. *Vigna's Archive*

Right: Close-up view of mechanics working on a *8° Stormo* SM79 at Castel Benito in Libya. *Vigna's Archive*

Below right: An F-84F Thunderstreak of the postwar *8° Stormo's 101 Gruppo*. This aircraft was restored by Captain Zaltron and other personnel of the Group, and it is now the gate guardian at Cervia AB. *Toselli and Grattoni Archives*

relatively uneventful year the *8° Stormo* was transferred to Sicily on 29 January 1943, being located first at Palermo and then at Chimisia San Giuseppe. The Axis forces were on the retreat in North Africa and by the time of the *Stormo*'s move to Sicily, Allied forces were well established in Algeria and the *Afrika Korps* had been forced back into Tunisia by the Eighth Army. In January, most of the *Regia Aeronautica* units in North Africa were withdrawn to Italy.

Successive changes of base by the *27°* and *28° Gruppi* were made in Sicily before the Allied invasion of the island on 10 July 1943, by when the *Stormo* had relocated to the mainland, the Wing HQ and the *27° Gruppo* going to Bologna and the *28° Gruppo* to Perugia. On 8 September, five days after the Anglo-American landings in Southern Italy, the *27° Gruppo* was disbanded. The following day, Mussolini having been overthrown, the Italian government announced an Armistice with the Allies. The *28° Gruppo* of the *8° Stormo* was disbanded a few days later, but in 1944 some of the Group's aircrews joined the Martin Baltimore-equipped *Stormo* of the embryo *Aeronautica Militare Italiana* operating with the Allies, particularly against the Axis forces in Yugoslavia.

More than two decades were to pass before the *8° Stormo* reappeared in the modern era, and it was on 14 September 1967 that the Wing re-formed at Cervia-San Giorgio. The *Stormo* was equipped with F-84F Thunderstreaks passed on by the *6° Stormo*. By this time the F-84Fs had been in *AMI* service for 11 years and were beginning to show their age. The eventual replacement aircraft to reach the *Stormo* was the Fiat G91Y, the modified, twin-engined version of the G91R with two General Electric J85 engines in place of the R's single Rolls-Royce Orpheus. The G91Y was noticeably up-armed with two 30mm DEFA cannon and four underwing stores hardpoints. In an effort to get the aircraft into service as quickly as possible, pilots and groundcrew of the *8° Stormo* were detached to the *AMI* flight test unit at Practica di Mare in order to help clear the acceptance trials on the G91Y.

At the beginning of 1971 the first three G91Ys arrived at Cervia bearing the Wing codes 8-01,-02 and -03. The remaining airworthy F-84Fs were passed to the *50° Stormo* and those aircraft in the worst condition were scrapped. The groundcrews' enthusiasm for the new aircraft found an outlet in the painting of a large sharkmouth motif on the engine intake of aircraft '03' but this unofficial marking was removed on orders from air force headquarters and the unit adopted a red lightning bolt as its emblem.

The advent of the G91Y brought the additional mission of reconnaissance to the Wing, which until then had operated in the fighter-bomber role. The aircraft is equipped with four cameras – one forward-looking, two oblique and one vertical – providing a 180 degree, panoramic coverage. In the reconnaissance role, the G91Ys of the *8° Stormo*

36619
8-34

8 01

effectively act as a back-up to the *AMI's* specialist fighter-reconnaissance Wing, the *3° Stormo Caccia Ricognitori* comprising the *28°* and *132° Gruppi CR* at Verona-Villafranca.

At Cervia, the *8° Stormo* is based less than 20 miles away from the *5° Stormo Caccia*, an F-104S Starfighter Wing, at Rimini-Miramare so all the training sorties of the two *Stormi* are co-ordinated to avoid traffic conflicts. Besides its recce activity, the *101° Gruppo* practises a fairly standard sequence of fighter ground-attack training making use of the air to ground ranges both onshore and off the Italian Adriatic coast. The 8th Wing base also houses an Operational Technical Service group which is responsible for the maintenance of the G91Ys and the regular overhaul of the aircraft at intervals of 25,50 and 100 flying hours. Major overhauls are conducted at 800hr intervals and for those the aircraft are sent to Naples, where the engines are also rectified – by Alfa Romeo.

Also part of the *8° Stormo* is a liaison flight for continuity training. This sub-unit is equipped with two-seat G91T training aircraft usually on detachment from the *AMI's* advanced flying training school at Foggia-Amendola.

Now well into the second decade of the operation with the *8° Stormo*, the Aeritalia G91Y has proved a popular aircraft with the unit – and a comparitively safe one to fly, only four aircraft having been written off since 1971.

Left: The first G91Y, 8-01, issued to the *8° Stormo* at the beginning of 1971. *Toselli and Grattoni Archives*

Below left: Close-up of an *8° Stormo* pilot in the cockpit of a G91Y – the emblem of the *101° Gruppo* is featured on his helmet and the side of the aircraft's fuselage. *Toselli and Grattoni Archives*

Below: A G91Y taxying past the flightline at Cervia AB; the aircraft carries the red lightning flash and emblem of the *101° Gruppo* below the cockpit and the badge of the *8° Stormo* on its fin. *Vigna's Archive*

Acknowledgement

The author would like to thank the Commander of Cervia-San Giorgio Air Base, the personnel of the 8° *Stormo* – in particular Captain Zaltron – for their help in compiling the article; and the 'Vigna' and 'Toselli-Grattoni' archives for assistance with the illustrations.

The 'Defunct Clunk' - a look back at the retirement of the CF-100

Philip M. Kitchen

A visit to the Northeastern United States and Canada during July and August of 1981 was designed to capture on film the passing of an era in military aviation in that area. Sad to recall, 1981 witnessed the phasing out of the B-57 from service with the 134th DSES at Burlington, Vt, the departure from service of the F-101B with the 138th TFS at Niagara Falls NY and, perhaps saddest of all, it was the year of the final demise of the CF100 Canuck. The last seven CF100s of No 414 EW Squadron, CFB North Bay, retired officially on 31 December 1981. With the passing of Canada's only indigenous fighter to see service, a chapter closed in the history of Canadian aviation.

In keeping with an aircraft of the significance and character of the CF100, steps were taken to ensure that it went out with a bang rather than a whimper. By mid-1980 the 'Defunct Clunk Club of Canada' had been formed with a view to organising a reunion of all those who had been connected with the aircraft either at the development stage or during squadron service. Membership was extended further to include those who were simply aviation enthusiasts who wished to mark the passing of the CF100 in a special way.

The club published a regular newsletter and items such as pens, tie-tacks and binders carrying a CF100 motif were made available for sale to members. A limited edition of prints of the CF100 was commissioned and a specially selected wine was bottled and distinctively labelled for the DCC of C.

The reunion took place between the evening of Thursday 10 September and the afternoon of Sunday 13 September 1981 with over 2,500 people in attendance. The highlight of the weekend was the air show staged on the Saturday afternoon and there are no prizes for guessing which aircraft stole the show.

Below: An air-to-air view of CF100, 100780; the shortened wing of the Mk 5D without the wingtip extensions is clearly seen here. *Canadian Forces*

The CF100 project was born in the immediate aftermath of World War Two. Growing Soviet airpower and increased tension between the US and the Soviet Union led the Canadian military to realize that Canadian airspace could be a major battleground in any future conflict. The RCAF put pressure on the Canadian government for a long-range, heavily armed, all-weather jet fighter that could operate in the Arctic. No such fighter was available at the time and so the Canadian aircraft industry set to work on its first fighter design. A Canadian engine, the Orenda, would be produced to power the new Canadian airframe.

The 19th January 1950 proved to be a significant date in Canadian aviation history. With Avro chief test pilot Bill Waterton at the controls, CF100 18101 took to the air. It was a striking all black aircraft with a white lightning streak painted along the side. It was powered by Rolls-Royce Avon engines because the Orenda was not yet available.

Over the next two years an extensive test programme was flown and an important stage in the development of the CF100 came on 11 October 1952. On that date the first operational CF100 Mk 3 flew. Powered by Orenda 8 engines and armed with eight

500
CANADA
500

476
CANADA

472
CANADA

.50 calibre Colt Browning machine guns in a retractable ventral pack, it was a very potent aircraft. The first Mk 3 was handed over to the RCAF on 15 August 1952. The CF100 training unit, No 3 All Weather Operational Training Unit, was formed at North Bay. The first squadrons to receive the Mk 3 were Nos 445,423 and 440.

On the same day as the Mk 3 prototype took to the air, so too did the Mk 4 prototype. This aircraft took much longer to reach the production stage because of the more protracted development of its weapons systems. It was equipped with the Hughes MG2 fire control system and the APG40 gun radar. The Mk 4 also had the distinctive wing tip rocket pods with 29 2.75in folding fin rockets in each pod. Aircraft performance was enhanced with the fitting of the Orenda 9 engine.

With the coming of the rocket equipped Mk 4 the 3 (AW) OTU moved from North Bay, Ontario to Cold Lake, Alberta. The ostensible reason for the move was that the greater range of the rockets required a large training area; most of the crews, however, were convinced that the move had more to do with the initial inaccuracy of the weapon, which was known to leave the pod anything between 30 degrees and 90 degrees from the direction of flight! Another hazard was the vibration set up by the machine guns. One pilot managed to shoot off his own nosewheel when vibration from the guns loosened rivets, causing a nose-wheel door to fall open and this in turn caused shells to be deflected into the nosewheel bay!

In all, 137 Mk 4A aircraft were built and these were joined later by 194 Mk 4Bs with Orenda 11 engines and an optional ventral rocket pack. The Mk 4B was to see service in Europe. In 1956 four CF100 squadrons replaced four of the RCAF Sabre units. No 445 Squadron joined No 1 Fighter Wing at Marville, No 423 Squadron joined No 2 Fighter Wing at Gros Tequin, No 440 Squadron joined No 3 Fighter Wing at Zweibrücken and No 419 Squadron joined No 4 Fighter Wing at Baden Söllingen. It was at this time too that the CF100 became a familiar sight at Prestwick where it underwent overhaul and maintenance at Scottish Aviation. The Prestwick connection was marked on 17 December 1981 when CF100 18784 – an ex No 414 Squadron Mk 5D in full 1950s style camouflage scheme – made two low passes over the airport on its way to Baden Söllingen.

The final version of the CF100 to see service with the RCAF was the Mk 5. This was a considerably re-worked aircraft with 3½ft extensions to each wingtip, a larger tail, new rocket pods containing 50 rockets, but the ventral guns were deleted. As well as seeing Canadian service, 53 Mk 5s were delivered to the Belgian Air Force from October 1957. They remained in service until 1964 when they were replaced by F-104s.

As events were to prove, the Mk 5 represented the swansong of the CF100. It was becoming obvious that more sophisticated weapons would be required for defence purposes. CARDE, the Canadian Armament Research and Development Establishment, began work on the Velvet Glove air-to-air missile, Canada's only indigenous missile design. Tests were begun in the early-1950s and they continued until 1957 when the project was abandoned in favour of the American built Sparrow 2 missile. It was hoped that the Mk 6 CF100 would go into service. This version would have been equipped with 4 Sparrow AAMs, but in fact the CF100 was superseded by the CF105 Arrow. The latter project, in turn, was abandoned and Canadian air defence came to rest on a combination of CF-101Bs, CF-104s and 56 Boeing Bomarc surface-to-air missiles. The CF100's career as an air defence fighter ended in 1963, but it was to continue in service in the reconnaissance, target towing and electronic warfare roles. It was in this last sphere that it continued in service until 1981.

The electronic warfare role developed in the RCAF in the mid-1950s. Initially DC-3s and a C-119 were used. In 1959 the RCAF's first official Electronic Warfare Unit was founded at St Hubert and by the mid-1960s the CF100 had become the mainstay of its equipment. On 15 September 1967 No 414 EW Squadron assumed the role of the RCAF's Electronic Warfare Unit and it has held that position ever since.

No 414 Squadron, the 'Black Knights', has had a varied career. Formed in Britain in 1941, the squadron performed reconnaissance, ground attack and forward air control duties during WW2. Aircraft types operated by the squadron included Lysanders, Tomahawks and Mustangs. Following WW2 the squadron went through a series of disbandments and re-formations and it appeared in various guises as a Dakota unit, a Sabre unit, a CF100 unit and CF-101B unit. It re-formed in its present EW role at St Hubert in 1967, transferred to Uplands in 1968 and finally re-located to its current base at North Bay, Ontario in 1972.

The CF100 variant used in the EW role was the CF100 Mk 5D. The ventral armament housing contained a package of electronic gear weighing over

Top left: No 414 Squadron's '500', with underwing chaff dispensers visible outboard of the engines.
Philip M. Kitchen

Centre left: Some idea of the size of CF100 can be gained from the height of the crew access ladder.
Philip M. Kitchen

Bottom left: The CF100's T-shaped dorsal jamming aerial, used in the EW training role, can be seen against the background of the hangar – a similar aerial also protruded from the lower fuselage.
Philip M. Kitchen

Above: The successor to the CF100 with No 414 Squadron was the EW-configured CC117 – note the jamming aerials forward of the wing and a chaff-dispensing chute below the tail. *Philip M. Kitchen*

Above right: The third type of aircraft operated by No 414 Squadron in recent years is the CT133 – this example is 'clean winged' but the aircraft can be fitted with underwing jamming or chaff dispenser pods. *Philip M. Kitchen*

Right: The aircraft which replaced the 'Clunk' in CF front-line fighter service was the CF101 Voodoo. This CF101B is shown in the markings of No 425 Squadron, the 'Alouettes', based at CFB Bagotville, Que. *Philip M. Kitchen*

1,000 lb. This fact combined with increased tankage brought the weight of the aircraft up to the 40,000 lb mark. Another distinguishing feature lay in the deletion of the wingtip extensions of the standard Mk 5. The wingtip rocket pods gave way to tip tanks, and chaff dispensers were fixed to underwing hardpoints. Just as the CF100 had been very potent in its fighter role, so too it was a very challenging opponent in the EW role. It had the capacity to jam both air and ground radars and communications. During its career it took part in countless exercises, the best known of which was the 'Maple Flag' series held at Cold Lake. The CF100 could always be relied upon to give any 'enemies' an unpleasant time.

As well as the CF100, No 414 Squadron operates CT-133s. These can be equipped with chaff dispensers or jamming pods on underwing mounts, but they do not perform the range of tasks of the CF100. The true successor of the CF100 in the EW role is the CC-117. Three of these aircraft were transferred from the VIP role with No 412 Squadron at Ottawa. They are equipped with an EW console in the starboard rear of the aircraft. To the author's knowledge at least one of the aircraft, 117507, has been modified to give it a chaff dispensing facility through a chute beneath the tail. The main external feature which permits the EW Falcon to be distinguished from its VIP counterpart is the provision of T-shaped aerials above and below the fuselage. These jamming aerials were also a prominent feature on the CF100.

It is believed that the other four CC-117 aircraft in Canadian Forces service will be modified for the EW role. They will represent a considerable advance on the present CC-117s in No 414 Squadron service. As well as updated cockpit avionics they will have more advanced EW equipment and provision for two Electronic Warfare Officers. As an interesting

footnote, it seems that there may have been a change in designation for the EW Falcon. The shoulder flashes worn by the crews carry a plan view of the aircraft and the legend EW-117.

On the day of the author's visit to North Bay all seven remaining CF100s were present, although only one CC-117 and seven CT-133s were seen. Clearly the aircraft of No 414 Squadron are heavily utilised in the EW training role. The following aircraft were noted:

CC-117 – 117507; **CT-133** – 133422, 133618, 133500, 133165, 133604, 133455 and 133491; **CF100** – 100790, 100504, 100784, 100500, 100742, 100746 and 100785.

Of the CF100s, two wore special paint schemes which had been applied as part of the celebrations. Aircraft 100784 was in 1950s style camouflage as already noted, but even more spectacular was 100785, resplendent in the full black scheme of the prototype. The CF100 was an aircraft with class and it went out in the same way it arrived.

Acknowledgement
The author would like to acknowledge his gratitude to the following whose help was invaluable in the preparation of this article: Lieutenant P.O'Connor, No 414 Squadron CF, Mr Adrian Holloway, Mr Gerald McLaughlin and Mr James Gemmell.

The McDonnell Douglas

WHEN in April 1963, the then Douglas Aircraft Co Inc announced its intention to develop and produce a twin-engined jet airliner, the DC-9, only the wildest optimists could have envisaged the scale to which the programme would grow. Indeed the project started off rather inauspiciously because the announcement of the new entrant to the 'Douglas Commercial' aircraft series, in succession to the four-jet DC-8, was made without the backing of a firm airline order. Nor could there have been any contemporary awareness that in a significant respect the DC-9 would be the last of its line – the final commercial transport to be developed by Douglas Aircraft Co; after a span of four decades from 1928, the famous aircraft manufacturer's separate corporate identity was to disappear in April 1967, when the Company merged with the McDonnell Company to form the McDonnell Douglas Corporation.

DC-9

But the foundations of the DC-9 programme had been well established by then and the remarkable evolution of the airliner was to be carried forward under the combined auspices of McDonnell Douglas with great effect; so much so that as the design passed its 20th anniversary, it had long since consolidated its position as the most successful twinjet transport in civil aviation history. By September 1982 there had accumulated firm orders for a total of 1,086 DC-9s of all models, plus 14 conditional orders and options which brought the order book up to a grand total of 1,100. Up to the beginning of September 1982 deliveries of DC-9s had amounted to 1,061 and these aircraft were in service with 74 operators around the world. The manufacturer's assessment of DC-9 utilisation indicates that the worldwide fleet provides services to more than 550 cities in 75 nations, each day completing over 6,000 flights and carrying nearly three million passengers per week. The DC-9 fleet had flown a cumulative 8,600 million miles, said McDonnell Douglas, and logged almost 25 million revenue-earning hours of flight time since entering airline service in 1965.

The distribution of the DC-9s around the world varies widely but, in September 1982, there were 11 airlines each with 30 aircraft or more who accounted for over half the aggregate number of McDonnell Douglas twinjets in service. The three largest operators of the DC-9 were US airlines – Republic Airlines Inc with no less than 129 DC-9s, Eastern Air Lines Inc with 79, and US Air Inc with 71. The largest offshore operators were Scandinavian Airlines System with 58, followed by Air Canada with 37 and Swissair with 32.

The announcement that the DC-9 programme was to be launched came on 8 April 1963; although the Douglas Aircraft Co had spent more than a year with a well-defined product aimed at the short-haul market, there had been no takers up to the time of the launch date and several more weeks were to pass before Delta Air Lines signed a contract in May 1963 for 15 aircraft with 15 more on option.

Top left: The first DC-9, N9DC, outside the Douglas Aircraft Co plant at Long Beach, Ca. The aircraft made its maiden flight on 25 February 1965.
All photos courtesy McDonnell Douglas Corp

Left: The scene at Long Beach, Ca some 16 years later as the Douglas Aircraft Co Division of McDonnell Douglas Corp effected the handover of the 1,000th DC-9, a Super 80 for Swissair. Standing to the left of the Super 80 was a DC-9 srs 10, the first model of the twinjet airliner, attesting to more than a decade and a half's development of the design.

The DC-9 was to be built in numerous versions, aimed at meeting a variety of operator requirements in terms of capacity and range – and also exploiting the growth possibilities conferred by aerodynamic and powerplant development – but the first of six major variants was the DC-9 series 10. The initial example, with the registration N9DC and powered by two Pratt & Whitney JT8D-5 engines rated at 12,000lb thrust each, made its maiden flight from Long Beach, Ca on 25 February 1965. In all, five srs 10 aircraft were involved in the subsequent flight trials of the DC-9 which were brought to a successful conclusion on 23 November 1965 with the award of the Federal Aviation Authority's (FAA) Type Approval. Delta Air Lines put the DC-9 into service two weeks later, on 8 December.

A total of 137 DC-9 srs 10s were built during the ensuing three years, these including four all-passenger versions (the srs 11, 12, 14 and 15) plus two convertible passenger/cargo models – the DC-9 srs 15 MC (multiple change) and the DC-9 srs 15 RC (rapid change). Both the latter had a strengthened main deck floor and side cargo door in the left forward fuselage, but the MC had folding passenger seats in the rear plus cargo in front, whereas the RC's seating was mounted on pallets for quick removal to create cargo space. In all-passenger configurations, the capacity of the srs 10 aircraft varied from 72 seats in a mixed class arrangement to 90 seats in a five-abreast, high density layout.

Although initially known as the DC-9B or DC-9 srs 20, the next version of the twinjet was to become the srs 30, with a fuselage length increased by 15ft to allow a maximum passenger complement of 115. The srs 20 designation was to be used on a later version of the airliner. The srs 30 first flew on 1 August 1966 and after achieving FAA certification in December of that year, the new variant started service with Eastern Air Lines in February 1967. Operating at higher weights than the srs 10, the srs 30 was given a 4ft wider wing span and field performance was boosted also by the adoption of full-span leading edge slats. Whereas the various models of srs 10 aircraft used JT8D engines in the power range 12-14,000lb, the srs 30s were initially powered by a pair of JT8D-9s giving 14,500lb each, and with subsequent increases in the maximum gross take-off weight of the series the engine options rose to the 16,000lb-rated JT8D-17s.

The next version of the DC-9 was the srs 40 – a stretched variant of the srs 30 with an additional fuselage length of over 6ft to accommodate up to 125 passengers. Evolved to meet a Scandinavian Airlines System requirement for a short range, high capacity aircraft the srs 40 first flew on 28 November 1967 entering service with SAS in 1968 and also being purchased by Toa Domestic Airlines of Japan;

The DC-9 srs 20 followed the srs 40 into the air after an interval of less than a year – the first aircraft making its maiden flight on 18 September 1968. This model of the DC-9 was ordered only by SAS for its 'domestic' operations in Scandinavia. Earmarked specifically for operations off short runways, the srs 20 had the fuselage and capacity of the srs 10 married to the longer, slatted wings of the srs 30, and it was powered by 14,500lb or 15,000lb versions of the P&W JT8D engine. The DC-9 srs 20 began service with SAS in January 1969.

The next version of the DC-9, and marking a significant further transformation of the aircraft, was the srs 50, which allied the long-span slatted wing of the srs 30 to a fuselage length stretched anew to 133ft 7in – the latter being some 14ft longer than that of the srs 30 and 8ft longer than the srs 40. The srs 50, with a maximum seating capacity of 139, first flew on 17 December 1974 and entered service with Swissair in August of the following year. Powered by -15 or -17 versions of the JT8D with thrust ratings of 15,500-16,000lb, the DC-9 srs 50 became the main production variant of the twinjet airliner in the latter half of the 1970s.

The sixth major version of the DC-9, announced in October 1977, was the series 80, or 'Super 80' as MDC labelled it. The aircraft, with new engines, a still longer fuselage and larger wings, went into production development after orders from Swissair and Austrian Airlines. Power for the Super 80 comes from two refanned Pratt & Whitney JT8D-209 engines rated at a take-off thrust of 18,500lb each, with an additional reserve of 750lb thrust available automatically to the good engine in the event of an engine-out condition on one of the powerplants. An alternative engine is the JT8D-217 of 20,000lb thrust with an automatic reserve of 850lb. The larger fans of the -209 engine confer improved fuel economy and lower noise characteristics. The Super 80's fuselage is over 14ft longer than that of the srs 50, allowing a maximum passenger complement of 172, and the aircraft's wing span was extended by over 14½ft compared with the srs 50. The Super 80's enlarged wing, it has a wing area 28 per cent greater than that of the srs 50, allows the carriage of an additional 1,520 US gal of fuel.

The Super 80 first flew on 18 October 1979 and received its FAA certification in August 1980, the airliner entering service with Swissair in October 1980. Up to 1 September 1982, MDC had received orders for 112 Super 80s, plus conditional orders and options for another 12 of the aircraft.

As well as the commercial operators of the DC-9, there are several military users of the twinjet transport, notably including the US Air Force and US Navy. The USAF flies an aeromedical evacuation version of the DC-9 srs 32 CF (convertible freighter) designated the C-9A Nightingale. This aircraft retains the CF's side cargo door but has a built-in stretcher loading ramp. The USAF also operates a VIP-transport version of the srs 30, the VC-9C. The US Navy DC-9 is the C-9B known as the Skytrain II; this is another version of the srs 32 CF's and flown by the USN and also the US Marine Corps.

Top: A DC-9 srs 15, N970Z, of the US regional carrier Ozark Air Lines.

Above: Air Canada has been a long-time and consistent operator of the DC-9 and today has the second largest fleet of the twinjets of any airline outside the US. The photo shows a DC-9 srs 10 in the Canadian flag carrier's livery.

Below: The srs 10 aircraft are still very much in active service – even with the newest airlines. This view shows a DC-9 srs 14 in the markings of Midway Airlines; the airline is headquartered at Chicago's Midway Airport, and it began operations in November 1979.

Above right: A DC-9 srs 14, OH-LYC, serving with Finland's national airline, Finnair Oy.

Right: Almost ready for delivery to Eastern Air Lines, note the airline's two-tone blue speed stripes along the fuselage, N8916E was still carrying the titles proclaiming the new series 30 version of the DC-9 at the time of this photo. The series 30 made its revenue earning debut with Eastern, in February 1967.

Below: A take-off view of '916', fully painted in its new owner's livery.

Above: A view of the DC-9 final assembly line at Long Beach, Ca with a double row of the twinjets stretching the length of the hall.

Below: This Iberia DC-9 srs 32, EC-BIG, was distinguished in carrying the name of the nation's capital city; in full, its name is *Villa de Madrid.*

Top right: A European airline which has been closely associated with the DC-9 since the earliest days of the programme is KLM. Shown here is one of the Dutch airline's srs 32s, *City of Istambul.*

Centre right: A DC-9 srs 31, N935VJ, of US Air, the name adopted by the former Allegheny Airlines in October 1979 to reflect the developing scale of the carrier's business.

Below: The DC-9 srs 40 embodied an additional fuselage stretch over the srs 30 and was evolved to meet the needs of Scandinavian Airlines System (SAS). This 'compressed' view of a srs 40 aircraft shows SAS' SE-DDT, named *Amund Viking.*

Below: The only other airline to purchase the specialised srs 40 aircraft, which was optimised to cover short-haul/high capacity requirements, was Toa Domestic Airlines (TDA) of Japan, whose JA8440 is seen here.

Bottom: Even more of a composite in the DC-9 programme was the srs 20, again developed for SAS. This version of the airliner combined the fuselage of the srs 10 with the high-lift wing of the srs 30 and the 14,500lb thrust engines of the srs 40.

Below: Another fuselage stretch and yet more powerful engines led to the srs 50 version of the DC-9; the prototype aircraft, N54641, was pictured at lift-off for its first flight on 17 December 1974. With the concurrent energy crisis beginning to bite, the new variant's improved fuel economy and reduced direct operating costs led to contemporary description of the srs 50 as the 'inflation fighter'.

Bottom: Flightdeck view of a DC-9 srs 50 on an approach to a US airport – the runway can be discerned through the centre panel of the windscreen.

Left: The handover of the first DC-9 srs 50 to the lead customer, Swissair, was marked on 14 August 1975. In front of the full size aircraft – c/n 47656, registered HB-ISM and named *Wettingen* – a scale model of the airliner was presented to Mr Robert Staubli, right, Swissair's vice president of flight operations, by Mr John C. Brizendine, president of the Douglas Aircraft Co. The Swiss airline also took delivery later the same year, in November, of the prototype srs 50 aircraft, c/n 47654, N54641, which became HB-ISK *Hori* in Swissair service.

Below: The US carrier North Central Airlines took delivery of its first DC-9 srs 50, N760NC, on 6 April 1976 as part of an order for six of the aircraft. The Minneapolis-headquartered airline later joined with Southern Airways of Atlanta, Ga in July 1979 to form Republic Airlines Inc; which itself subsequently took over Hughes Airwest in 1980. Republic is now the largest DC-9 operator in the world, with 129 of the twinjet airliners in service during late-1982.

Bottom: A side view of a DC-9 srs 50 at Long Beach, Ca in May 1976 just before its delivery to the Yugoslav airline Inex Adria Airways.

Left: As the sign proclaimed, this was the nose section of the first DC-9 Super 80 under construction at Long Beach in November 1978. A year earlier, after obtaining firm orders from Swissair and Austrian Airlines for this further stretched version of the DC-9, the manufacturer had initiated production development work on the Super 80.

Below: The result of the Super 80 development programme takes to the sky for the first time; the prototype aircraft, N980DC, was seen getting airborne from Long Beach at the start of its maiden flight on 18 October 1979.

Bottom: A late-1981 'new look' interior for the Super 80 featuring enlarged baggage racks and a simulated 'wide cabin' ceiling. Deliveries of the new interior configuration began in the spring of 1982.

Above: Comparative view of the Super 80 and srs 30 versions of the DC-9 seen together at Schiphol Airport, Amsterdam in late-1981. The Dutch airline, Martinair, leased the Super 80, YU-ANB, from Inex Adria ahead of the delivery of its own aircraft, scheduled for early-1983. Shortly after obtaining 'ANB' on lease, Martinair relinquished one of its own srs 30 aircraft, PH-MAX, a srs 33RC, seen in the background here.

Below: A DC-9 srs 82 of Air Cal, N478AC, The airline operates a fleet of Super 80s and Boeing 737s on services between points in California, Nevada, Washington and Arizona.

Build it yourself

Below: One of the oldest homebuilt designs still being constructed is the Luton LA-4 Minor. The first prototype flew in 1937 and examples have been built ever since. Single-seat and of wood construction, the Luton Minor is a good first project for the homebuilder; this immaculate example, G-AXKH, first flew on 22 June 1974. *Unless otherwise credited, all photos: Andrew P. March*

A. P. March

HOME-BUILDING is very well established in the UK and there are up to 600 projects under way at any given time. All homebuilt projects in this country are handled by the Popular Flying Association (PFA). This is a non-profit making organisation charged with the mechanics of design, manufacture and certification of homebuilts since the last war. There have been many changes since the ultra-light projects of the early post-war years, such as Turbulents, Luton Minors and Tipsy Nippers. The PFA now handles homebuilts up to 180 hp, vintage restorations and types of aircraft that cannot be handled by the Civil Aviation Authority, which is necessarily orientated to general and commercial aviation.

The control of homebuilts, complete or incomplete is based upon a small, full time staff of volunteers at the PFA Headquarters, Shoreham Airport. As well as providing technical support to the homebuilder through its team of inspectors, the PFA also sponsors group flying. Basically this is a number of people who join together to operate an aircraft as a group. In this way standing charges such as hangarage and insurance can be shared. A vital part of the PFA's activities involves the influencing of legislation, to the benefit of the pilots and home-builders. The strength of its position comes from its independence from other aviation agencies and influences.

The range of aircraft that can be built under the PFA umbrella is huge. The types are restricted to the following criteria: maximum power 180 hp; maximum weight 1,000 kg all up; maximum of 2 seats and stalling speed of 60 mph or less. Within this, keeping in mind that the power can be arranged with either one or two engines, just about anything can be built from the diminutive Colibri through tourers such as Jodels and Emeraudes, to racers such as the Cassutt and aerobatic aircraft like the Pitts Special.

From the airframe point of view the types of constuction vary from the traditional wood and fabric aircraft, through metal and fibreglass right up to the latest composite materials made popular in recent years by the designs of American Burt Rutan and seen in this

Top: Luton Major, G-ASWH, in its original form with a Walter Mikron engine. *Peter R. March*

Above: One of the most popular homebuilt aircraft in Europe is the Rollason D.31 Turbulent. Using a converted Volkswagen engine, the D.31 was first produced in 1958. This example, G-AWDO, first flew in 1969 and now has a three-blade propeller.

Left: The compact Monnet Sonnerai II, a tandem seat, low wing tail dragger with a steel tube and fabric constuction fuselage and all-metal wings. G-BOBY is registered appropriately to Robert Hallam and has PFA No 15 – 10223.

Top: A truly fine replica of recent years is the Sopwith Tabloid, G-BFDE, constructed by Don Cashmore. The aircraft is painted in a Royal Navy colour scheme and carries the serial 168. The amount of work necessary to produce such an unusual and immaculate homebuilt as this is evident from the photo.

Above: The classic, fully aerobatic Pitts Special biplane first flew in 1944 yet it is still a favourite in the aerobatic world, available in two basic types – the single-seat S-1 and the tandem seat S-2. The Pitts S-1S, illustrated here, has ailerons on the upper and not the lower wing; it is the standard aerobatic version and this one carries a very appropriate registration.

Top: The Brugger MB.2 Colibri II is a small, all-wood, single-seat monoplane. First flown in 1970, the Colibri is stressed for aerobatics and is suited to engines in the VW1600 class. This example was built by Brian Perkins in Bristol, hence the G-BPBP registration.

Left: The Evans VP-1 has become very popular in the UK and there are a comparatively large number flying. Of extremely simple construction, the VP-1 makes an ideal first project for beginners. This particularly neat example, seen at the PFA International Rally at Cranfield in 1982, is based in Scotland.

Bottom left: The second British-built example of the Steen Skybolt, G-BGRT; this is a very popular design in the United States, and the two-seat biplane is fully aerobatic, being stressed to +12G/−10G.

Right: The single-seat Tipsy Nipper, G-AWLS, shows off its simple design in this take-off view. This example was factory built although a number of homebuilt examples are currently flying. *Peter R. March*

Below right: The Replica Plans SE5A, G-BDWJ, carries the RAF serial number, F8010. Built to the Canadian company's design, this replica was constructed by Mike Beach, is powered by a Continental C90 engine, and was first flown in 1978.

country in the distinctive form of the VariEze. The obvious engine choice is the Lycoming or Continental, however they are by no means the only ones available. Modified car engines such as the Volkswagen are very popular and as long as specificatons such as dual ignition are met the sky is the limit!

The quality of your workmanship must meet certain standards laid down by the PFA. At stages in construction your appointed inspector will ensure that the aircraft is well made from good materials and will ultimately be airworthy.

Before setting off on the long and possibly arduous path of constructing your own aircraft the potential home-builder is advised to look over the many types of aircraft that he could choose from. Many of the homebuilt aircraft types can be seen flying and on the ground at the PFA International Rally, held at Cranfield, Beds over the first week in July each year. There are also many smaller PFA Strut events held up and down the country throughout the summer months. These will give you the opportunity of talking to PFA home-builders and pilots about the advantages and disadvantages of particular designs and structures. You will find that they will be able to give you all sorts of hints and tips and advice in large measure.

Your problem is deciding which aircraft, powerplant and construction method will suit you, your pocket and experience best from the huge variety available. And if you are not contemplating building your own light aircraft you will still find it fascinating to look at the high standards of finish and construction achieved by the enthusiasts who have built their own Pitts, Condor, Luton Major, Great Lakes, Sonerai or Acrosport, or such fine replicas as the SE5A, Spitfire, Mustang, Sopwith Tabloid and Focke-Wulf FW190 to name but a few from the growing catalogue. Make no mistake, PFA homebuilt aircraft are real flying machines built to exacting specifications and designed to last. They should not be confused with home constructed microlights which mirror the experimental products of the pioneer days of flying before World War 1.

Above: Among a number of homebuilt scale replica aircraft flying is the six-tenths scale Isaacs Spitfire. An all-wood aircraft, this example, G-BBJI is powered by a Rolls-Royce Continental 0-200-A. This aircraft is the prototype and first flew from Thruxton in early-1975. To the time of writing, it was the only example on the register.

Below: The Rutan VariEze is proving to be a popular design in the UK. Built of glass fibre filled with urethane foam the aircraft has many novel features, including the canard layout, large winglets and retracting nosewheel – the latter to facilitate access to the cockpit.

'Coronets' in camera

SINCE 1975 the US Air Force has been running an annual series of short-term, trans-Atlantic deployments from the Continental US to Western Europe by tactical fighter units of Tactical Air Command (TAC) and TAC-gained Air Force Reserve (AFRES) and Air National Guard (ANG) formations. These deployments, generally of two-three weeks' duration, are part of a wider programme in which US-based units have also deployed to the Western Pacific and Alaska in order to familiarise aircrews with the very different aspects of operations outside the CONUS. The deployment exercises in this series are codenamed with a 'Coronet' prefix, and in Europe their purpose has been to test the reinforcement of US Air Forces in Europe's (USAFE) in-place tactical airpower permanently assigned to the Command's three numbered air forces – 3rd AF, 16th AF, and 17th AF. During the early phase of the 'Coronet' series exercises to Europe in the mid-1970s it was apparent that the deployment destinations mainly featured USAFE's established main operating bases (MOBs). But with the successful growth of the Command's endeavours to establish a pattern of additional, co-located operating bases (COBs) on which USAF aircraft would operate alongside host nation air forces, the spread of the deployments was widened; and the purpose of the exercises became more specifically geared to providing US-based squadrons with experience of the European bases from which they would have to operate in a war situation.

The accompanying photographs show some of the aircraft and locations featured in recent 'Coronet' exercises, and the other aircraft that support the deployments by providing air-to-air refuelling facilities for the tactical fighters, airborne command and control of the deployments and re-deployments, airlift of maintenance personnel and equipment, and en route search and rescue coverage. In addition, there follows a description of an individual exercise, 'Coronet Wrangler', which took place in early-1982.

Above: Typical of the supporting tankers making possible the rapid deployment of CONUS-based USAF tactical aircraft to Europe is this KC-135A Stratotanker. Pictured at RAF Mildenhall, this KC-135, s/n 58-0043, is operated by the 133rd Air Refueling Squadron, 157th Air Refueling Group of the New Hampshire Air National Guard. Based at Pease AFB, NH the aircraft was one of the KC-135s that accompanied the 'Coronet Mil' deployment across the Atlantic. *Cambridge Aviation Photographers*

Right: The appropriately named 'Coronet Eagle' deployment, 2 October-5 November 1980, brought F-15 Eagles of the 58th TFS/33rd TFW from Eglin AFB, Fl to Bremgarten AB, Germany, where one of the F-15As, s/n 77-0079, is seen landing. *Rainer Karras*

Left: The 93rd Tactical Fighter Squadron of the 915th Tactical Fighter Group, US Air Force Reserve, flew 12 of its F-4C Phantoms from Homestead AFB, Fl to Bodo AB, Norway in January 1982 at the start of a deployment codenamed 'Coronet Mil'. The non-stop flight from Florida to Northern Norway was supported by KC-135 Stratotankers, and the second 'cell' of six F-4Cs of the 93rd TFS is seen here astern of one of the Stratotankers during an air-to-air refuelling rendezvous at 28,00ft en route to Norway. *Cambridge Aviation Photographers*

Left: The badge of the 474th TFW.

'Coronet' Wrangler

Mike Taylor

THE 474th Tactical Fighter Wing's 429th Tactical Fighter Squadron from Nellis AFB, Nv deployed to RAF Bentwaters, Suffolk – home of USAFE's A-10 equipped 81st TFW, during late-April 1982. The exercise, codenamed 'Coronet Wrangler', was designed to familiarise the F-16 Fighting Falcon crews with the European operating environment.

The 429th TFS deployed 11 single-seat F-16As and one two-seat F-16B to Bentwaters, their arrival marking the first time the F-16 had been deployed in strength to the United Kingdom. The aircraft flew non-stop from Nellis and were refuelled by four Boeing KC-135A tankers over the Continental US and were then accompanied across the Atlantic by two McDonnell Douglas KC-10A Extender tankers of the 2nd Bomb Wing and a Boeing EC-135K Tactical Command Post of the 8th Tactical Deployment Control Squadron, which is used to control movements of fighter aircraft overseas. The F-16s made an average of seven hook-ups each with the tanker aircraft on their 10½hr flight. Approximately 200 personnel supported the exercise with some of the ground crews and equipment being flown in by a Lockheed C-5A Galaxy and Lockheed C-141B Starlifters.

While temporarily based at Bentwaters the aircraft flew both high and low-level navigational flights within the United Kingdom and Europe. Practice bombing runs were made with 4, 6 and 25lb stores on ranges in the Netherlands, Denmark and the UK. Air Combat Training (ACT) missions were also flown in the West German ACT areas with F-15 Eagle aircraft of the 36th Tactical Fighter Wing from Bitburg AB, West Germany. Dissimilar Air Combat Training was also carried out with the 'aggressor' squadron based at RAF Alconbury, Cambridgeshire, the DACT training with the F-5Es of the 527th TFTAS taking place in the North Sea ACT zone.

Bottom: Groundcrew preparing a 429th TFS F-16A, s/n 79-0399, for a rapid turnround after the aircraft's return to Bentwaters from a low-level navigation and attack training sortie over the UK. *Cambridge Aviation Photographers*

Above: McDonnell Douglas KC-10A Extender cargo/ tanker aircraft provided air refuelling support for the F-16s on the trans-Atlantic leg of their 10½hr flight to the UK.

Below: Two-seat F-16B of the 429th TFS undergoing pre-flight checks while an A-10A Thunderbolt II of the Bentwaters-based 81st TFW comes into land in the background. Note the presentation of the F-16's s/n, 79-429th! *USAF, Audio Visual Section RAF Bentwaters*

Top: 'Coronet Heron' in June 1978 involved the deployment of USAF Tactical Air Command RF-4C Phantoms of the 363rd Tactical Reconnaissance Wing from Shaw AFB, SC to RAF Coltishall, Norfolk. *Cambridge Aviation Photographers*

Above: In the same month, June 1978, another Norfolk base, RAF Sculthorpe, was the destination for US Air Force Reserve F-105D Thunderchiefs of the 465th TFS/507th TFG from Tinker AFB, Ok taking part in 'Coronet Oriole'. This aircraft, s/n 59-1729 carried the title *East Anglian Express* on its nosewheel door. *Cambridge Aviation Photographers*

Above: July 1978 saw a three-week visit to RAF Wittering, codenamed 'Coronet Teal', by A-7D Corsair IIs of the Air National Guard drawn from three different units – the South Carolina Air Guard's 157th TFS/169th TFG, the 166th TFS/121st TFW of the Ohio Air Guard, and the Pennsylvania Air Guard's 146th TFS/112nd TFG. This South Carolina ANG A-7D carried the Guard's US Bicentennial badge below and behind the cockpit, plus an emblem with the title *War Eagle V.*
Cambridge Aviation Photographers

Below: Another multi-unit ANG A-7D Corsair deployment took place the following year when, in August 1979, aircraft of the Iowa and South Dakota Air Guards were detached to RAF Waddington for 'Coronet Stallion'. This view shows two A-7Ds of the 124th TFS/132nd TFW Iowa Air National Guard landing at Waddington. *P. A. Rowings*

Below: A less frequent visitor to Europe on the 'Coronet' deployments than the A-7 or F-4 is the F-111. 'Coronet Hammer' in May-June 1980 saw F-111Ds of the 522nd TFS/27th TFW from Cannon AFB, NM detached to the A&AEE airfield at Boscombe Down, Wilts. One of the 'CC' fin-coded aircraft on the deployment, s/n 68-0122, was pictured at RAF Greenham Common during the Newbury Air Festival, held on 31 May-1 June.
Cambridge Aviation Photographers

Bottom: An Air National Guard RF-4C Phantom deployment to RAF Alconbury in September 1980 was 'Coronet Gyro', which brought the 153rd TRS/186th TRG from Meridian, Ms. One of the squadron's aircraft, painted in the two-tone green and tan camouflage with matt finish and 'wrapped around' to extend to the lower surfaces as well as the upper surfaces, was pictured on the taxiway at Alconbury. The visit to Alconbury was a last minute change of plan as the Mississippi Air Guard Phantoms had been scheduled to deploy to Larissa AB, Greece under the 'Coronet Gyro' plan.
Cambridge Aviation Photographers

Top: Seen at Bremgarten AB, West Germany – home base of the *Luftwaffe's* RF-4E Phantom Wing *AKG51* 'Immelmann' – in October 1980, an F-15B Eagle of the 58th TFS/33rd TFW from Eglin AFB, Fl taking part in the appropriately codenamed 'Coronet Eagle' deployment. *Rainer Karras*

Above: A four-ship F-15 sortie on the runway at Bremgarten ready for take-off at the start of a training sortie during 'Coronet Eagle'. *Rainer Karras*

Above: 'Coronet Mast' in March 1981 featured a deployment by the 113th TFS/181st TFG of the Indiana ANG from Terre Haute, in to Andoya AB, Norway. The 'HF'-coded F-4C Phantoms of the squadron were obliged to make an en route diversion to Alconbury owing to poor weather in Norway. *Cambridge Aviation Photographers*

Above right: In June 1981 Air National Guard A-7D Corsairs were back in the UK, and on this occasion the 125th TFS/138th TFG from Oklahoma visited RAF Wittering during 'Coronet Canvas'. *P. A. Rowlings*

Right: F-4Cs of the 93rd TFS/915th TFG AFRES en-route from Homestead AFB, Fl to Bodo AB, Norway at the start of the early-1982 'Coronet Mil' deployment. *Cambridge Aviation Photographers*

Below: Among the aircraft supporting the 'Coronet Mil' deployment was this airborne command post Boeing EC-135K of the 8th Tactical Deployment Control Squadron from Tinker AFB, Ok. *Cambridge Aviation Photographers*

Bottom: Also invariably brought to stand-by in support of the trans-Atlantic 'Coronet' deployments are the search and rescue assets of USAF Military Airlift Command, whose HH-53 helicopters and HC-130 Hercules of the 67th Aerospace Rescue and Recovery Squadron operate from RAF Woodbridge, Suffolk with a detachment based at Keflavik AB, Iceland. Seen at Woodbridge is one of the 67th ARRS HC-130N Hercules. *Cambridge Aviation Photographers*

Right: An F-4C Phantom of the 110th TFS/131st TFW Missouri ANG from St Louis, Mo at RAF Leeming in mid-1982 during the 'Coronet Cactus' deployment which took place from 26 June – 10 July. *Cambridge Aviation Photographers*

Below: Landing at RAF Finningley in June 1982, an F-4D Phantom of the Illinois Air National Guard's 183rd TFG. Twelve of the Group's F-4Ds took part in 'Coronet Brave' between 12-25 June deployed from their home base at Springfield, Il. *Crown Copyright, RAF Finningley*

Below: Supporting the 'Coronet Brave' deployment were C-141B Starlifters of Military Airlift Command, which brought the 183rd TFG's equipment and some 300 personnel to RAF Finningley for the two-week detachment. One of the C-141Bs, from the 437th Military Airlift Wing, is seen at Finningley. *Crown Copyright, RAF Finningley.*